CW00566455

X-Rated Cocktails

Steve Quirk

NEW HOLLAND

CONTENTS

INTRODUCTION

There is a cocktail to suit every occasion, from fun with friends to intimate and naughty celebrations with your significant other, you will soon master the skills to mix cheeky cocktail concoctions using these delicious recipes. This book provides a specific range of adult X-Rated cocktails and mixed drinks that will liven up any party, whether it's a Bucks night or Hens night or even just a group of friends that want to have fun with a few drinks and a good laugh. If you are meeting for a few drinks before hitting the town for a celebration, then these drinks will get you excited and in the mood for a great night out.

There are 269 X-Rated cocktail recipes at your fingertips to select from, ensuring there is a drink name for every naughty mood. Be warned, it's not for the faint hearted, so if you've ever fancied *sex on the beach* but never quite been brave enough, this book is here to immerse you into a world of wild dreams and fantasies.

Why not host a naughty themed party and really have your guests blushing and laughing as they call out what they would like. The reactions could be very entertaining as you call out such drink names as "who wants a Blow Job or an Orgasm" then watch them come running.

So *Get Between the Sheets* and *Get Laid*, with a *Comfortable Screw*, and release your *Creamy Orgasm* with these easy to follow cocktail recipes, it's time to have a little naughty fun!

Approximate % alcohol volume (% alc/vol) content has been calculated and supplied for each drink containing alcohol within this book, as well as how many standard drinks each contains. These calculations are based on information obtained that is believed to be accurate and reliable, although cannot be guaranteed due to % alc/vol variations between the different brands of spirits and liqueurs. These calculations should only be used as a guide.

The % alc/vol for all spirits and liqueurs required for drinks contained within this book are provided in the glossary – if unsure then compare your spirits and liqueurs with the % alc/vol provided in the glossary.

COCKTAILS ARE WHAT?

The cocktail's origin is unknown, although there are many theories of how the word originated. One such theory is that during the American Revolution, in Betsy's Tavern, a French man toasted 'vive le cocktail' after sighting bottles or glasses decorated with bird feathers by bartender Betsy Flanagan. Another theory is that the word originated from the practice of docking a horse's tail (cocktail) for mixed breeds as opposed to thoroughbreds, although I fail to see the connection between a horse's tail and a drink.

A more appropriate definition of a cocktail is a drink containing two or more ingredients served in glasses of various shapes and sizes. They are shaken, stirred, built, layered or blended.

CONSTRUCTING A COCKTAIL

Shaking – When ingredients are required to be shaken, half fill a cocktail shaker with ice, and then pour ingredients into the shaker. This will chill the ingredients quicker than pouring the ingredients into shaker before the ice. Avoid over-filling your shaker – leave room for shaking. To shake, stand still and shake vigorously for about ten seconds, strain into chosen glass and serve or garnish. The majority of cocktail shakers have a strainer; if yours does not then you can use a hawthorn strainer. Effervescent drinks should never be shaken in a cocktail shaker. Rinse shaker out thoroughly after each use and dry with a clean lint-free cloth. This will ensure that your drinks only have in them what they are supposed to and will not distort the flavor of the next drink that you prepare.

Stirring – Where ingredients are required to be stirred, half fill a mixing glass with ice and pour the ingredients over the ice. Stir and strain into chosen glass. Usually ingredients that mix easily together are prepared in this manner.

Building – To build a drink is to pour ingredients in order given into a highball glass over ice and serve with a swizzle stick for the recipient to admire and stir.

Layering – To layer a drink is to pour ingredients in order given (pour over the back of a spoon into chosen glass). This will allow the liquid to flow down the inside rim of glass, creating a layering effect. Usually the heavier ingredients are poured first.

Blending – When a blender is required, only use cracked or crushed ice in suitable blenders and blend until ingredients are evenly mixed.

Cocktails should be drunk as soon as they are served.

USEFUL TIPS

Frosting – This is for the purpose of coating the rim of a glass with salt or sugar. This is achieved by moistening the rim of a glass using a slice of lemon or orange. Then hold the chosen glass by its base or stem upside down and rest gently on a flat plate containing salt or caster sugar and twist slightly. If you press down on glass too hard, this may result in chunks of salt or sugar sticking to the rim. Lemon is used for salt-frosted rims and orange for sugar-frosted rims unless otherwise stated.

Sugar syrup – For the sugar syrup mix together 225 g (8 oz) of ordinary white sugar with 240 ml (8 fl oz) of water and almost bring to the boil in a small saucepan stirring continuously, simmer until the sugar is completely dissolved. Then remove from heat and allow to cool. Once cool, pour into a re-sealable container or a corked bottle and store in refrigerator or behind your bar for regular use. This syrup will now last indefinitely.

Sweet and sour mix – For a sweet and sour mix bring 240 ml (8 fl oz) of sugar syrup to simmer then add 120 ml (4 fl oz) of fresh lemon juice and 120 ml (4 fl oz) of fresh lime juice. Simmer till well mixed stirring frequently, then remove from the heat and allow to cool. Once cool, pour into a re-sealable container or a corked bottle and store in the refrigerator for up to one to two weeks. Sweet and sour mix is also refered to as sour mix or bar mix.

To chill a glass – Glasses can be chilled by placing them into a refrigerator or by placing ice cubes into the glasses while drinks are being prepared. Discard these ice cubes before pouring unless otherwise instructed.

Fruit, peels and juices – Fruit slices and pieces will keep fresher and longer if covered with a damp clean linen cloth and refrigerated. Where citrus peel is required, cut the peel into required sizes and shave away the white membrane. Fruit and peels should be the last added ingredient to a cocktail (garnish). When juices are required remember – fresh is best. When using canned fruit and/or juices, transfer the can's contents into appropriate re-sealable containers and refrigerate.

Ice – It is important to maintain a well-stocked clean ice supply, as most cocktails require ice during construction. To obtain crushed ice if you do not have access to an ice-crushing machine, place required ice onto a clean linen cloth and fold up. Place ice-filled cloth onto a hard surface and smash with a mallet – (not a bottle).

GLASSWARE

Glasses come in a wide variety of shapes and sizes and range in value depending upon the quality of glass. When washing glasses, use hot water without detergent as detergent can distort the flavor of a drink or reduce the fizz in an effervescent drink. Only wash one glass at a time and dry with a clean lint-free cloth. Before using a glass, give it a quick polish with a glass cloth and check glass for chips and/or cracks. When handling glassware, hold glasses by their base or stem, as this will avoid finger marks around the rim of the glass, thus maintaining a high polish.

The following is a compiled list of glassware required for cocktails within this book, although for the home bar an extensive range of glassware is not always necessary. As an example, a wine glass could be used as a cocktail glass.

Beer	210 ml (7 fl oz) – 375 ml (13 fl oz)
Brandy Balloon	240 ml (8 fl oz) – 750 ml (26 fl oz)
Champagne Flute	140 ml (4 fl oz) – 180 ml (6 fl oz)
Champagne Saucer	140 ml (4 fl oz) – 180 ml (6 fl oz)
Cocktail	90 ml (3 fl oz) – 140 ml (4 fl oz)
Coffee	250 ml (8 fl oz)
Collins	360 ml (12 fl oz)
Cordial	30 ml (1 fl oz) – 90 ml (3 fl oz)
Goblet	140 ml (4 fl oz) – 285 ml (9½ fl oz)
Highball	300 ml (10 fl oz)
Hurricane	230 ml (7 fl oz) – 650 ml (21 fl oz)

Liqueur	30 ml (1 fl oz) – 90 ml (3 fl oz)
Margarita	260 ml (8 fl oz)
Old-Fashioned	180 ml (6 fl oz) – 290 ml (9 fl oz)
Sherry/Port	60 ml (2 fl oz) – 120 ml (4 fl oz)
Shot	30 ml (1 fl oz) – 60 ml (2 fl oz)
Tall	360 ml (12 fl oz)
Wine	150 ml (5 fl oz) – 210 ml (7 fl oz)

MEASURES

1 Dash 1 ml ($\frac{1}{30}$ fl oz)
1 Teaspoon 5 ml ($\frac{1}{6}$ fl oz)
1 Tablespoon 18 ml ($\frac{3}{5}$ fl oz)

BAR EQUIPMENT

Before purchasing any bar equipment, have a search through your kitchen as the majority of households contain a selection of items required for your bar. The following is a list of the basic essential equipment.

Bottle Opener	Cutting Board	Knives	Stirrers
Bottle Stoppers	Fruit Juicer	Mixing Glass	Straws
Blender	Glass Cloth	Napkins	Swizzle Sticks
Can Opener	Hawthorn	Soda Siphon	Toothpicks
Coasters	Strainer	Spirit Measure	
Cocktail Shaker	Ice Bucket and	Sponge	
Corkscrew	Tongs	Spoons	

YOUR OWN BAR

Before you buy your bar, it is advisable to visit pubs, clubs, cocktail bars or friends that may have home bars. By doing this, it will assist in providing you with a broader spectrum on what sort of bar would best suit you. This will also provide you with ideas on lighting, what they have in common and what appeals to you personally. Also take into consideration how much room you have for a bar and your budget. There are many different sizes and styles of bars. The three main categories are:

Mobile Bar – The purpose of a mobile bar is that it can be moved easily to a position from which you wish to serve, e.g., room to room or indoors to outdoors.

Semi-Permanent Bar – This is a bar that is a main feature of a room to be intended as a showpiece where glassware and bottles can be displayed. This style of bar should be erected close to washing up facilities.

Permanent Bar – A permanent bar can turn a room into a bar room containing a built-in sink behind the bar with hot and cold water, a fridge/freezer, equipment and accessories. Glass shelving with mirrored backing provides the opportunity to place your glassware and bottles on display. Mood lighting can be used to great effect in such a room. Adding a couple of matching bar stools and a couple of lounges makes for the perfect room to retire to after that long day's work, not to mention cocktail parties that you could hold in style.

COMMON INGREDIENTS FOR COCKTAILS

SPIRITS

Bacardi

Bourbon

Brandy

Campari

Canadian Whisky

Cognac

Dark Rum

Gin

Irish Whiskey

Light Rum

Malibu

Port

Scotch Whisky

Sherry

Southern Comfort

Tennessee Whiskey

Tequila

Vodka

LIQUEURS

Advocaat

Amaretto

Bailey's Irish Cream

Banana Liqueur

Bénédictine

Cherry Brandy

Cointreau

Crème De Cacao

Crème De Cassis

Crème De Menthe

Curaçao

Drambuie

Frangelico

Galliano

Grand Marnier

Kahlúa

Midori

Strawberry Liqueur

Tia Maria

COMMON MIXERS

Apple Juice	Eggs	Passion-Fruit Nectar
Apricot Nectar	Grapefruit Juice	Pineapple Juice
Bitter-Lemon Soda	Honey	Soda Water
Bitters	Lemonade	Sweet and Sour Mix
Coconut Cream	Lemon Juice	Tabasco Sauce
Coconut Milk	Lime Juice	Tonic Water
Coffee	Lime Syrup	Vanilla
Cola	Mango Juice	Vanilla Ice Cream
Cranberry Juice	Milk	Water (spring)
Cream	Orange Juice	
Dry Ginger Ale	Passion-Fruit Juice	

COMMON GARNISHES AND ADDITIVES

Bananas	Lemons	Pineapple
Butter	Limes	Salt
Cinnamon	Maraschino Cherries	Sprigs of Mint
Cocktail Umbrellas	Melon	Strawberries
Grated Chocolate	Oranges	Sugar
Hazelnuts	Passion-Fruit	
Kiwi Fruit	Peaches	

CORDIALS AND LIQUEURS

Cordials and liqueurs are alcohol-based with herbs, aromatic plants, essences, juices, beans, nuts, dairy products, sweeteners and colors which are infused in the spirit by the process of steeping and distillation.

Cordials and liqueurs date back centuries, in 1510 Bénédictine DOM was created by a Benedictine monk making it one of the world's oldest known liqueurs. The recipe for Bénédictine still remains a closely guarded secret as is the case for many cordials and liqueurs.

Traditionally, cordials and liqueurs were created for medicinal purposes as a cure for all types of ills. Creating cordials and liqueurs hundreds of years ago meant that people would gather herbs, fruits and plants from their gardens and then added them with sugar to liquors such as: Gin, Brandy and other liquors. Today cordials and liqueurs are produced by distilling companies worldwide. It would not be possible to list all cordials and liqueurs that are being produced or available. A list has been provided of the main ones that are required for cocktails contained within this book in the introduction.

Cordials and liqueurs are essential ingredients in a vast variety of cocktails.

BRANDY

Naughty Brandy drinks include: *Bare Naked Lady* – (pays to advertise), *Jack Me Off* – (for the lazy guys), *Wet One* – (she's ready), *Just Feel* – (getting started) and *Naughty Night* – (gotta love those).

Brandy is distilled from grapes (another useful use of grapes besides just eating them) and is produced in the majority of Wine-producing nations around the world.

Cognac is a fine smooth Brandy produced in Charente, France and is arguably defined as the world's finest Brandy. For a bottle to be labelled Cognac, the grapes must be grown, fermented and distilled in the region of Charente.

Fruit Brandies are Brandy-based liqueurs with a wide variety available.

The quality markings for Brandy and Cognac are as follows:

VSOP (very superior old pale)

VSO (very superior old)

VOP (very old pale)

*** (three stars)

** (two stars)

* (one star)

MANEATER

36.6% alc/vol
1.8 standard drinks

45 ml (1 ½ fl oz) Brandy
15 ml (½ fl oz) Southern Comfort
2 dashes Orange Bitters

Pour ingredients into a cocktail shaker over ice and shake. Strain into an old-fashioned glass over crushed ice and serve.

SEX IN A BUBBLEGUM FACTORY

12.1% alc/vol
2.6 standard drinks

30 ml (1 fl oz) Apricot Brandy
30 ml (1 fl oz) Banana Liqueur
30 ml (1 fl oz) Curaçao
30 ml (1 fl oz) Light Rum
150 ml (5 fl oz) Lemon-Lime Soda

Pour Brandy, Liqueur, Curaçao and Rum into a mixing glass over ice. Stir and strain into a chilled highball glass. Add soda, stir gently and serve.

BAREFOOT AND PREGNANT

31.6% alc/vol
1.5 standard drinks

30 ml (1 fl oz) Brandy
15 ml (½ fl oz) Dry Vermouth
10 ml (⅓ fl oz) Maraschino Liqueur
5 ml (⅙ fl oz) White Crème De Menthe

Pour ingredients into a cocktail shaker over ice and shake. Strain into a chilled cocktail glass and serve.

BARE NAKED LADY

8.7% alc/vol
1.4 standard drinks

30 ml (1 fl oz) Apple Brandy
30 ml (1 fl oz) Bacardi Black
90 ml (3 fl oz) Sweet and Sour Mix
60 ml (2 fl oz) Fresh Orange Juice

Pour ingredients into a cocktail shaker over ice and shake. Strain into a highball glass over ice and serve.

JACK ME OFF

14.1% alc/vol
1.7 standard drinks

45 ml (1½ fl oz) Applejack
15 ml (½ fl oz) Midori
90 ml (3 fl oz) Lemonade

Pour Applejack and Midori into a cocktail shaker over cracked ice. Shake and pour into a chilled highball glass. Add lemonade, stir gently and serve.

POP THE CHERRY

4% alc/vol
0.8 standard drinks

45 ml (1½ fl oz) Cherry Brandy
210 ml (7 fl oz) Fresh Orange Juice
Cherry
Slice of Orange

Pour Brandy and juice into a chilled highball glass over a few ice cubes then stir. Garnish with a cherry and slice of orange then serve.

BOSOM CARESSER

27% alc/vol
2.3 standard drinks

60 ml (2 fl oz) Brandy
30 ml (1 fl oz) Orange Curaçao
5 ml (⅙ fl oz) Grenadine
Yolk of 1 Egg

Pour ingredients into a cocktail shaker over ice and shake. Strain into a chilled cocktail glass and serve.

WET ONE

27.8% alc/vol
1.8 standard drinks

60 ml (2 fl oz) Brandy
10 ml (⅓ fl oz) Fresh Lime Juice
2 teaspoons Orgeat Syrup
Wedge of Lime

Pour Brandy, juice and syrup into a cocktail shaker over ice. Shake and strain into a chilled cocktail glass. Garnish with a wedge of lime and serve.

FRENCH ORGASM

31.4% alc/vol
3 standard drinks

75 ml (2½ fl oz) Cognac
45 ml (1½ fl oz) Bailey's Irish Cream

Pour ingredients in order given into a brandy balloon, swirl gently and serve.

JUST FEEL

13.5% alc/vol
1.7 standard drinks

40 ml (1 fl oz) Cognac
23 ml (¾ fl oz) Apricot Brandy
40 ml (1 fl oz) Grape Juice
40 ml (1 fl oz) Fresh Orange Juice
15 ml (½ fl oz) Strawberry Syrup

Pour ingredients into a cocktail shaker over ice and shake. Strain into a chilled tall glass over a few ice cubes and serve.

HORNY MONK

36% alc/vol
1.9 standard drinks

45 ml (1½ fl oz) Cognac
23 ml (¾ fl oz) Amaretto

Pour ingredients into a cocktail shaker over ice and shake. Strain into an old-fashioned glass filled with ice and serve.

DIRTY MOTHER

32.8% alc/vol
1.6 standard drinks

45 ml (1½ fl oz) Brandy
15 ml (½ fl oz) Kahlúa

Pour ingredients into an old-fashioned glass filled with ice, stir and serve.

WHO'S YA DADDY

33.4% alc/vol
2.4 standard drinks

60 ml (2 fl oz) Cognac
30 ml (1 fl oz) Kahlúa

Pour ingredients into a cocktail glass over ice, stir and serve.

FRENCH WHORE

33.3% alc/vol
1.6 standard drinks

30 ml (1 fl oz) Cognac
30 ml (1 fl oz) Tia Maria

Pour ingredients into a cocktail glass, stir and serve.

NAUGHTY
NIGHT

31.2% alc/vol
1.8 standard drinks

30 ml (1 fl oz) Cognac
30 ml (1 fl oz) Port
15 ml (½ fl oz) Grand Marnier

Pour ingredients into a mixing glass without ice and
stir. Pour into a port glass and serve.
This drink was created by the author of this book.

TASTY ONE

31.5% alc/vol
3 standard drinks

60 ml (2 fl oz) Apricot Brandy
60 ml (2 fl oz) Bénédictine

Pour ingredients into a tall glass over ice,
stir and serve.

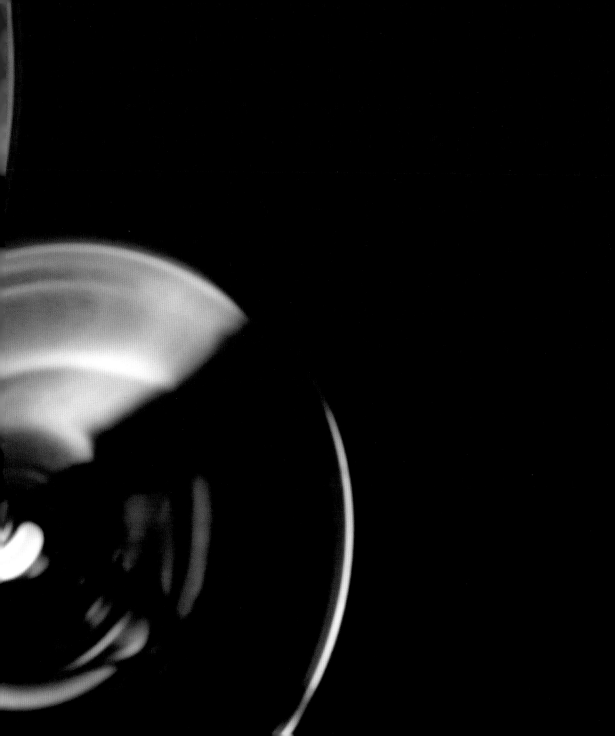

GIN

Naughty Gin drinks include: *Love in an Elevator* – (going down), *Lucky Stiff* – (being satisfied), *Virgin* – (still waiting) and *Wet Dream Cocktail* (waking to a wet mess).

Gin originated from Holland in the 17th century when a Dutch physician produced Gin using juniper berries and alcohol for medicinal purposes. It is funny how medicine has changed over the years and now we are advised not to mix alcohol with medications, go figure.

Today Gin is produced by distilling grain mash such as barley, corn and rye in column stills. This neutral spirit is then combined with water to reduce the strength before being redistilled with botanicals and aromatics. The botanicals and aromatics required for this procedure are primarily juniper berries and coriander. Other botanicals and aromatics that are used by distillers include bitter almonds, caraway seeds, cinnamon, fennel, ginger, lemon

and orange peel, roots and other secret ingredients.
Gin is an unaged spirit with London Dry Gin being the most common type of Gin and is produced by distillers around the world.

MISTRESS

12.4% alc/vol
2 standard drinks

45 ml (1½ fl oz) Gin
30 ml (1 fl oz) White Crème De Cacao
60 ml (2 fl oz) Pineapple Juice
30 ml (1 fl oz) Passion-Fruit Juice
30 ml (1 fl oz) Thick Cream
5 ml (⅙ fl oz) Campari
Maraschino Cherry

Pour Gin, Cacao, juices and cream into a cocktail shaker over ice. Shake and strain into a highball glass over ice. Add Campari by gently pouring on top – do not stir, then garnish with a cherry and serve.

BROWN PUSSY

30.6% alc/vol
1 standard drink

20 ml (⅔ fl oz) Dry Gin
10 ml (⅓ fl oz) Dark Crème De Cacao
10 ml (⅓ fl oz) Triple Sec

Pour ingredients into a cocktail shaker over ice and shake. Strain into a chilled cocktail glass and serve.

RUSTED ROOT

13.6% alc/vol
1.7 standard drinks

60 ml (2 fl oz) Gin
8 ml (¼ fl oz) Fresh Lemon Juice
1 teaspoon Sugar Syrup
White of 1 Egg
60 ml (2 fl oz) Root Beer

Pour Gin, juice, sugar and egg white into a cocktail shaker over ice. Shake and strain into a collins glass over ice. Add root beer and stir gently. Add more ice to fill glass and serve.

WET DREAM COCKTAIL

27.5% alc/vol
1 standard drink

30 ml (1 fl oz) Gin
8 ml (¼ fl oz) Apricot Brandy
8 ml (¼ fl oz) Grenadine
Dash Fresh Lemon Juice

Pour ingredients into a cocktail shaker over ice and shake. Strain into a chilled cocktail glass and serve.

LUSTY LUCY

8.3% alc/vol
1.4 standard drinks

30 ml (1 fl oz) Gin
30 ml (1 fl oz) Midori
30 ml (1 fl oz) Grapefruit Juice
1 teaspoon Egg White
113 ml (3¾ fl oz) Tonic Water
3 Melon Balls (various colors)

Pour Gin, Midori, juice and egg white into a cocktail shaker over ice. Shake and strain into a chilled highball glass. Add tonic and stir gently. Garnish with melon balls and serve.

VIRGIN

33.4% alc/vol
2 standard drinks

30 ml (1 fl oz) Gin
30 ml (1 fl oz) Forbidden Fruit
15 ml (½ fl oz) White Crème De Menthe

Pour ingredients into a cocktail shaker over ice and shake. Strain into a chilled cocktail glass and serve.

SUGAR DADDY

25.1% alc/vol
2 standard drinks

60 ml (2 fl oz) Gin
10 ml (⅓ fl oz) Maraschino Liqueur
Dash Angostura Bitters
30 ml (1 fl oz) Pineapple Juice

Pour ingredients into a cocktail shaker over ice and shake. Strain into a chilled cocktail glass and serve.

BLUE BALLZ

30.1% alc/vol
1.4 standard drinks

30 ml (1 fl oz) Gin
15 ml (½ fl oz) Blue Curaçao
15 ml (½ fl oz) Midori

Pour ingredients into a cocktail shaker over ice and shake. Strain into an old-fashioned glass over ice and serve.

WOMANIZER

27.7% alc/vol
1.5 standard drinks

40 ml (1 fl oz) Genever Gin
10 ml (⅓ fl oz) Cherry Brandy
10 ml (⅓ fl oz) Parfait Amour
2 teaspoons Lime Syrup
Twist of Lemon Peel

Pour Gin, Brandy, Parfait Amour and syrup into a cocktail shaker over ice. Shake and strain into a chilled cocktail glass. Add lemon peel and serve.

LOVE IN AN ELEVATOR

16.5% alc/vol
2.3 standard drinks

60 ml (2 fl oz) Gin
30 ml (1 fl oz) Blue Curaçao
90 ml (3 fl oz) Soda Water

Pour Gin and Curaçao into a cocktail shaker over cracked ice. Shake and pour into a chilled collins glass. Add soda, stir gently and serve.

SWEATY BALLS

24.3% alc/vol
1.4 standard drinks

23 ml (¾ fl oz) Gin
23 ml (¾ fl oz) Apricot Brandy
23 ml (¾ f l oz) Dry Vermouth
5 ml (⅙ fl oz) Fresh Lemon Juice
Maraschino Cherry

Pour Gin, Brandy, Vermouth and juice into a cocktail shaker over ice. Shake and strain into a chilled cocktail glass. Garnish with a cherry and serve.

MAIDEN-NO-MORE

23.5% alc/vol
1.8 standard drinks

45 ml (1½ fl oz) Gin
15 ml (½ fl oz) Triple Sec
5 ml (⅙ fl oz) Brandy
30 ml (1 fl oz) Fresh Lemon Juice

Pour ingredients into a cocktail shaker over ice and shake. Strain into a chilled cocktail glass and serve.

SEX ROUGE

4.8% alc/vol
0.9 standard drinks

30 ml (1 fl oz) Gin
Dash Grenadine
100 ml (3 fl oz) Fresh Orange Juice
100 ml (3 fl oz) Dry Ginger Ale

Pour Gin, Grenadine and juice into a highball glass over ice then stir. Add ginger ale, stir gently and serve.

LUCKY STIFF

15.6% alc/vol
3 standard drinks

60 ml (2 fl oz) Gin
60 ml (2 fl oz) Orange Curaçao
120 ml (4 fl oz) Cranberry Juice

Pour ingredients into a highball glass over ice, stir and serve.

FORBIDDEN

28.2% alc/vol
2.7 standard drinks

30 ml (1 fl oz) Gin
30 ml (1 fl oz) Cognac
30 ml (1 fl oz) Forbidden Fruit
30 ml (1 fl oz) Fresh Lemon Juice

Pour ingredients into a blender over cracked ice and blend. Pour into a chilled champagne flute and serve.

DIRTY VIRGIN

33.6% alc/vol
1.6 standard drinks

45 ml (1½ fl oz) Gin
15 ml (½ fl oz) Dark Crème De Cacao

Pour ingredients into a cocktail shaker over ice and shake. Strain into an old-fashioned glass over ice and serve.

RUM

Naughty Rum drinks include: *Last Fling* – (about to be married), *Vegas Blowjob* – (what happens in Vegas stays in Vegas) and *Just a Gigolo* – (always happy to go to work).

Rum is distilled from fermented sugarcane and is produced by most sugarcane growing countries. There are three main types of Rums: White (light), Gold and Black (dark). Light Rums originated from the southern Caribbean Islands and are usually only aged for approximately one year in oak casks. Dark Rum has a richer stronger flavor than Light Rum.

Christopher Columbus introduced the West Indies to sugarcane and the first distilled sugarcane was produced for medicinal purposes as was the case with Gin.

By the 17th century Rum had become the drink issued to slaves who worked the plantations, I guess that was one way to keep them happy on the job, then by the mid-17th century, the Royal Navy crewmen were supplied a daily issue of Rum. This daily issue of Rum was to help battle the cold and scurvy.

BALL-CLENCHER

12.4% alc/vol
1.3 standard drinks

30 ml (1 fl oz) Dark Rum
15 ml (½ fl oz) Vodka
Dash Banana Liqueur
90 ml (3 fl oz) Pineapple Juice

Pour ingredients into a cocktail shaker over ice and shake gently. Strain into a chilled old-fashioned glass over a few ice cubes and serve.

BOOTY JUICE

33.2% alc/vol
1.4 standard drinks

15 ml (½ fl oz) Spiced Rum
15 ml (½ fl oz) Malibu
15 ml (½ fl oz) Midori
8 ml (¼ fl oz) 151-Proof Bacardi

Pour ingredients into a mixing glass over ice and stir. Strain into a chilled old-fashioned glass and serve.

DRY HOLE

6.6% alc/vol
1.6 standard drinks

30 ml (1 fl oz) Light Rum
15 ml (½ fl oz) Apricot Brandy
15 ml (½ fl oz) Cointreau
15 ml (½ fl oz) Fresh Lemon Juice
240 ml (8 fl oz) Soda Water

Pour Rum, Brandy, Cointreau and juice into a cocktail shaker over ice. Shake and strain into a tall glass over crushed ice then stir. Add soda, stir gently and serve.

LONG HARD ONE

52.9% alc/vol
7.5 standard drinks

90 ml (3 fl oz) 151-Proof Rum
30 ml (1 fl oz) Butterscotch Schnapps
30 ml (1 fl oz) Peach Schnapps
30 ml (1 fl oz) Rumplemintz

Pour ingredients into a cocktail shaker over ice and shake. Strain into a chilled highball glass and serve.

PLAYBOY COOLER

11.2% alc/vol
1.8 standard drinks

38 ml (1¼ fl oz) Golden Jamaica Rum
38 ml (1¼ fl oz) Tia Maria
90 ml (3 fl oz) Pineapple Juice
10 ml (⅓ fl oz) Fresh Lemon Juice
30 ml (1 fl oz) Cola
Slice of Pineapple

Pour Rum, Tia and juices into a cocktail shaker over ice. Shake and strain into a collins glass over ice. Add cola and stir gently. Garnish with a slice of pineapple and serve.

SEX ON THE BOAT

7.2% alc/vol
1 standard drink

30 ml (1 fl oz) Spiced Rum
8 ml (¼ fl oz) Banana Liqueur
135 ml (4½ fl oz) Fresh Orange Juice

Pour ingredients into a highball glass over ice, stir and serve.

CUBAN SCREW

12.3% alc/vol
1.7 standard drinks

60 ml (2 fl oz) Light Rum
120 ml (4 fl oz) Fresh Orange Juice
Maraschino Cherry
Slice of Orange

Pour Rum into a highball glass over ice and add juice then stir. Garnish with a cherry and slice of orange then serve.

HEAVENLY SEX

27% alc/vol
3 standard drinks

60 ml (2 fl oz) Spiced Rum
60 ml (2 fl oz) Amaretto
15 ml (½ fl oz) Grenadine
1 teaspoon Chocolate Syrup

Pour ingredients into a mixing glass over ice and stir well. Strain into a chilled champagne saucer and serve.

RANDY ANDY

14.4% alc/vol
1.5 standard drinks

45 ml (1½ fl oz) Light Rum
10 ml (⅓ fl oz) Banana Liqueur
30 ml (1 fl oz) Grapefruit Juice
30 ml (1 fl oz) Guava Juice
10 ml (⅓ fl oz) Fresh Lime Juice
2 teaspoons Passion-Fruit Syrup
Wedge of Lime

Pour Rum, Liqueur, juices and syrup into a cocktail shaker over ice. Shake and strain into a chilled cocktail glass. Garnish with a wedge of lime and serve.

SPERM BANK

22.8% alc/vol
1.6 standard drinks

45 ml (1½ fl oz) Light Rum
15 ml (½ fl oz) White Crème De Menthe
30 ml (1 fl oz) Fresh Cream

Pour ingredients into a cocktail shaker over ice and shake. Strain into a chilled cocktail glass and serve.

CALL-GIRL

8.3% alc/vol
1.7 standard drinks

15 ml (½ fl oz) Bacardi
15 ml (½ fl oz) Banana Liqueur
15 ml (½ fl oz) Coconut Liqueur
15 ml (½ fl oz) Dark Rum
15 ml (½ fl oz) Midori
90 ml (3 fl oz) Fresh Orange Juice
90 ml (3 fl oz) Pineapple Juice

Pour ingredients into a cocktail shaker over ice and shake. Strain into a chilled highball glass and serve.

TIGHT SNATCH

6.9% alc/vol
1.3 standard drinks

30 ml (1 fl oz) Light Rum
23 ml (¾ fl oz) Peach Schnapps
180 ml (6 fl oz) Pineapple Juice

Pour Rum and Schnapps into a mixing glass over ice. Stir and strain into a highball glass over ice. Add juice, stir well and serve.

SEX UNDER THE SUN

22.1% alc/vol
1.3 standard drinks

30 ml (1 fl oz) Bacardi
15 ml (½ fl oz) Dark Jamaica Rum
Dash Grenadine
15 ml (½ fl oz) Fresh Orange Juice
15 ml (½ fl oz) Pineapple Juice
Cherry
Twist of Lime Peel
Cocktail Umbrella

Pour Bacardi, Rum, Grenadine and juices into a cocktail shaker over cracked ice. Shake and pour into a chilled tall glass. Garnish with a cherry, lime peel and a cocktail umbrella then serve.

LAST FLING

10.9% alc/vol
0.9 standard drinks

10 ml (⅓ fl oz) Bacardi
10 ml (⅓ fl oz) Banana Liqueur
10 ml (⅓ fl oz) Cherry Brandy
10 ml (⅓ fl oz) Triple Sec
30 ml (1 fl oz) Fresh Orange Juice
30 ml (1 fl oz) Pineapple Juice

Pour ingredients into a cocktail shaker over ice and shake. Strain into a highball glass over ice and serve.

SPICE ORGASM

7.3% alc/vol
0.9 standard drinks

20 ml (⅔ fl oz) Spiced Rum
20 ml (⅔ fl oz) Banana Liqueur
60 ml (2 fl oz) Fresh Milk (chilled)
60 ml (2 fl oz) Banana Purée

Pour Rum, Liqueur and milk into a cocktail shaker over ice then add the purée. Shake well and strain into a highball glass half filled with crushed ice then serve.

SEX, LIES AND VIDEO POKER

17.7% alc/vol
1.3 standard drinks

15 ml (½ fl oz) Light Rum
15 ml (½ fl oz) Amaretto
15 ml (½ fl oz) Blended Whiskey
15 ml (½ fl oz) Grenadine
15 ml (½ fl oz) Fresh Orange Juice
15 ml (½ fl oz) Pineapple Juice

Pour ingredients into a cocktail shaker over ice and shake. Strain into a chilled cocktail glass and serve.

THINK PINK

4.1% alc/vol
0.9 standard drinks

20 ml (⅔ fl oz) Light Rum
20 ml (⅔ fl oz) Passoã
240 ml (8 fl oz) Lemon-Lime Soda

Pour Rum and Passoã into a mixing glass over ice. Stir and strain into a chilled highball glass. Add soda, stir gently and serve.

LOVE SHACK

16.4% alc/vol
1.1 standard drinks

38 ml (1¼ fl oz) Dark Rum
8 ml (¼ fl oz) Grenadine
10 ml (⅓ fl oz) Fresh Orange Juice
30 ml (1 fl oz) Lemonade

Pour Rum, Grenadine and juice into a cocktail shaker over ice. Shake and strain into an old-fashioned glass over ice. Add lemonade, stir gently and serve.

JUST A GIGOLO

22.6% alc/vol
1.1 standard drinks

30 ml (1 fl oz) Bacardi
10 ml (⅓ fl oz) Cherry Brandy
20 ml (⅔ fl oz) Pineapple Juice
Slice of Lemon

Pour Bacardi, Brandy and juice into a cocktail shaker over ice. Shake and strain into a chilled cocktail glass. Garnish with a slice of lemon and serve.

VEGAS BLOWJOB

23.7% alc/vol
1 standard drink

15 ml (½ fl oz) Light Rum
15 ml (½ fl oz) Jägermeister
8 ml (¼ fl oz) Banana Liqueur
8 ml (¼ fl oz) Fresh Orange Juice
8 ml (¼ fl oz) Pineapple Juice

Pour ingredients into a cocktail shaker over crushed ice and shake well. Pour into a chilled old-fashioned glass and serve.

TOUCHIE FEELIE

28.4% alc/vol
1.8 standard drinks

45 ml (1½ fl oz) Light Rum
15 ml (½ fl oz) Brandy
10 ml (⅓ fl oz) Fresh Lemon Juice
2 teaspoons Passion-Fruit Syrup

Pour ingredients into a blender over crushed ice and blend. Pour into a chilled champagne flute and serve.

HAWAIIAN
SCREW

12.5% alc/vol
1.8 standard drinks

30 ml (1 fl oz) Light Rum
30 ml (1 fl oz) Vodka
60 ml (2 fl oz) Fresh Orange Juice
60 ml (2 fl oz) Pineapple Juice

Pour ingredients into an old-fashioned glass over ice, stir well and serve.

SKINNY TART

8.9% alc/vol
1.1 standard drinks

38 ml (1¼ fl oz) Dark Rum
60 ml (2 fl oz) Grapefruit Juice
60 ml (2 fl oz) Pineapple Juice

Pour ingredients into a blender over crushed ice and blend. Pour into a chilled highball glass and serve.

VODKA

Naughty Vodka drinks include: *After Sex* – (we all need a drink after sex), *Sex Up Against the Wall* – (when you just can't wait), *Bend-Me-Over* – (one way to stretch your back) and *Losing Your Cherry* – (remember when you lost yours?).

 Vodka translates as "little Water" and originated from Eastern Europe around the 14th century, perhaps even earlier. Traditional Russian Vodka is distilled from potatoes with fruit or herbs added during the distilling process to provide a hint of flavor to the Vodka – one of the best uses for the humble potato.

 Today Vodka is used extensively in cocktails for improving the "kick" in a drink without disturbing the flavor. Perfect when added to your favorite fruit juice.

MISSILE RIDER

27% alc/vol
1.7 standard drinks

45 ml (1½ fl oz) Vodka
10 ml (⅓ fl oz) Yellow Chartreuse
3 dashes Pernod
20 ml (⅔ fl oz) Fresh Lime Juice
½ teaspoon Sugar Syrup

Pour ingredients into a cocktail shaker over ice and shake. Strain into a chilled old-fashioned glass and serve.

AFTER SEX

2.8% alc/vol
0.6 standard drinks

15 ml (½ fl oz) Vodka
8 ml (¼ fl oz) Banana Liqueur
240 ml (8 fl oz) Fresh Orange Juice

Prepare a tall glass with a sugar frosted rim - moistened with Grenadine then add a few ice cubes. Add Vodka and Liqueur then stir. Add juice, stir and serve.

SEXUAL TRANCE

17.6% alc/vol
1.3 standard drinks

30 ml (1 fl oz) Citrus Vodka
15 ml (½ fl oz) Chambord
15 ml (½ fl oz) Midori
15 ml (½ fl oz) Fresh Orange Juice
15 ml (½ fl oz) Pineapple Juice
5 ml (⅙ fl oz) Sweet and Sour Mix
Cherry

Pour Vodka, Chambord, Midori, juices and sour mix into a cocktail shaker over ice. Shake and strain into a highball glass over ice. Garnish with a cherry and serve.

HAWAIIAN SEDUCTION

10.7% alc/vol
1.8 standard drinks

30 ml (1 fl oz) Vodka
30 ml (1 fl oz) Tequila
150 ml (5 fl oz) Fresh Lime Juice

Pour ingredients into a highball glass over ice, stir and serve.

SEX ON THE BEACH WITH A CALIFORNIA BLONDE

6.9% alc/vol
1.3 standard drinks

30 ml (1 fl oz) Vodka
15 ml (½ fl oz) Chambord
15 ml (½ fl oz) Midori
90 ml (3 fl oz) Cranberry Juice
90 ml (3 fl oz) Pineapple Juice

Pour ingredients into a highball glass over ice, stir well and serve.

SEX ON THE BEACH

24.3% alc/vol
2.3 standard drinks

30 ml (1 fl oz) Vodka
30 ml (1 fl oz) Cointreau
30 ml (1 fl oz) Passoã
30 ml (1 fl oz) Fresh Orange Juice

Pour ingredients into a cocktail shaker over ice and shake. Strain into a chilled cocktail glass and serve.

LOVE JUICE

7.2% alc/vol
0.8 standard drinks

15 ml (½ fl oz) Vodka
15 ml (½ fl oz) Passion-Fruit Liqueur
8 ml (¼ fl oz) Pisang Ambon
45 ml (1½ fl oz) Fresh Orange Juice
45 ml (1½ fl oz) Pineapple Juice
15 ml (½ fl oz) Grenadine

Pour Vodka, Liqueur, Pisang Ambon and juices into a cocktail shaker over ice. Shake and strain into a highball glass over ice. Add Grenadine by pouring into centre of drink – do not stir, then serve.

BEND-ME-OVER

9.3% alc/vol
1.5 standard drinks

30 ml (1 fl oz) Vodka
30 ml (1 fl oz) Amaretto
120 ml (4 fl oz) Fresh Orange Juice
30 ml (1 fl oz) Sweet and Sour Mix

Pour ingredients into a highball glass over ice, stir well and serve.

PLEASURE SHIVER

18.9% alc/vol
1.3 standard drinks

15 ml (½ fl oz) Vodka
15 ml (½ fl oz) Amaretto
15 ml (½ fl oz) Triple Sec
15 ml (½ fl oz) White Crème De Cacao
30 ml (1 fl oz) Fresh Cream
Cinnamon

Pour Vodka, Amaretto, Triple Sec, Cacao and cream into a cocktail shaker over ice. Shake and strain into a chilled cocktail glass. Sprinkle cinnamon on top and serve.

PASSCACK VALLEY ORGASM

30.5% alc/vol
1.4 standard drinks

30 ml (1 fl oz) Vodka
15 ml (½ fl oz) Amaretto
15 ml (½ fl oz) Kahlúa

Pour ingredients into a cocktail shaker over ice and shake. Strain into a chilled highball glass and serve.

SEX ON
THE FARM

6.4% alc/vol
0.8 standard drinks

8 ml (¼ fl oz) Vodka
8 ml (¼ fl oz) Amaretto
8 ml (¼ fl oz) Malibu
8 ml (¼ fl oz) Midori
8 ml (¼ fl oz) Peach Schnapps
Dash of Grenadine
60 ml (2 fl oz) Fresh Orange Juice
60 ml (2 fl oz) Pineapple Juice
Cherry

Pour Vodka, Amaretto, Malibu, Midori, Schnapps, Grenadine and juices into a cocktail shaker over ice. Shake and strain into a chilled highball glass. Garnish with a cherry and serve.

100%
EXTASCY

27% alc/vol
1.3 standard drinks

30 ml (1 fl oz) Vodka
30 ml (1 fl oz) Bailey's Irish Cream

Pour ingredients into a mixing glass over ice and stir. Strain into a chilled cocktail glass and serve.

TROPICAL SCREW

6.6% alc/vol
1.2 standard drinks

30 ml (1 fl oz) Vodka
15 ml (½ fl oz) Triple Sec
180 ml (6 fl oz) Fresh Orange Juice
Wedge of Lemon

Pour Vodka, Triple Sec and juice into a highball glass over ice then stir. Garnish with a wedge of lemon and serve.

SEX ON THE BEACH WITH A FRIEND

19.6% alc/vol
2.8 standard drinks

45 ml (1½ fl oz) Vodka
45 ml (1½ fl oz) Crème De Cassis
45 ml (1½ fl oz) Midori
45 ml (1½ fl oz) Pineapple Juice

Pour ingredients into a mixing glass over cracked ice and stir. Pour into a chilled highball glass and serve.

JUST GOT LUCKY

7.5% alc/vol
1.2 standard drinks

40 ml (1 fl oz) Vodka
Dash of Banana Liqueur
100 ml (3 fl oz) Grapefruit Juice
60 ml (2 fl oz) Soda Water
Cherry
Slice of Pineapple

Pour Vodka, Liqueur and juice into an old-fashioned glass over ice then stir. Add soda and stir gently. Garnish with a cherry and a slice of pineapple then serve.

GOLDEN SCREW

12.5% alc/vol
1.3 standard drinks

45 ml (1½ fl oz) Vodka
Dash of Angostura Bitters
90 ml (3 fl oz) Fresh Orange Juice

Pour ingredients into a highball glass filled with ice, stir and serve.

QUICK FINNISH

19.6% alc/vol
1.8 standard drinks

30 ml (1 fl oz) Finlandia Vodka
23 ml (¾ fl oz) Quetsch
5 ml (⅙ fl oz) Dark Rum
60 ml (2 fl oz) Cola

Pour Vodka, Quetsch and Rum into an old-fashioned glass over ice then stir. Add cola, stir gently and serve.

SCREW IN THE TROPICS

9.3% alc/vol
1.8 standard drinks

60 ml (2 fl oz) Vodka
120 ml (4 fl oz) Fresh Orange Juice
60 ml (2 fl oz) Pineapple Juice

Pour ingredients into a cocktail shaker over ice and shake. Strain into a chilled highball glass over a few ice cubes and serve.

LOSING YOUR CHERRY

9.5% alc/vol
1.6 standard drinks

45 ml (1½ fl oz) Vodka
15 ml (½ fl oz) Cherry Brandy
90 ml (3 fl oz) Sweet and Sour Mix
60 ml (2 fl oz) Lemonade

Pour Vodka, Brandy and sour mix into a mixing glass over ice. Stir and strain into a chilled old-fashioned glass. Add lemonade, stir gently and serve.

ITALIAN SCREW

12.1% alc/vol
2.1 standard drinks

45 ml (1½ fl oz) Vodka
30 ml (1 fl oz) Galliano
180 ml (6 fl oz) Fresh Orange Juice

Pour Vodka and Galliano into a chilled highball glass over a few ice cubes then stir. Add juice, stir and serve.

HORNY LEPRECHAUN

15.6% alc/vol
2.8 standard drinks

45 ml (1½ fl oz) Vodka
45 ml (1½ fl oz) Midori
45 ml (1½ fl oz) Peach Schnapps
90 ml (3 fl oz) Fresh Orange Juice

Pour ingredients into a blender over crushed ice and blend until smooth. Pour into a chilled highball glass and serve.

SEX UP AGAINST THE WALL

9.3% alc/vol
0.9 standard drinks

30 ml (1 fl oz) Vodka
30 ml (1 fl oz) Cranberry Juice
30 ml (1 fl oz) Pineapple Juice
30 ml (1 fl oz) Sweet and Sour Mix

Pour ingredients into a cocktail shaker over ice and shake. Strain into a chilled highball glass and serve.

TORNADO ORGY

30.2% alc/vol
1.8 standard drinks

30 ml (1 fl oz) Vodka
15 ml (½ fl oz) Bailey's Irish Cream
15 ml (½ fl oz) Grand Marnier
15 ml (½ fl oz) Kahlúa

Pour ingredients into a cocktail shaker over ice and shake. Strain into a chilled cocktail glass and serve.

FRENCH SCREW

13.4% alc/vol
2.5 standard drinks

60 ml (2 fl oz) Vodka
60 ml (2 fl oz) Chambord
120 ml (4 fl oz) Fresh Orange Juice

Pour ingredients into a highball glass over ice, stir well and serve.

GET LAID

8.9% alc/vol
1.2 standard drinks

30 ml (1 fl oz) Vodka
23 ml (¾ fl oz) Raspberry Liqueur
120 ml (4 fl oz) Pineapple Juice
5 ml (⅙ fl oz) Cranberry Juice

Pour Vodka and Liqueur into a highball glass over ice. Add pineapple juice and stir. Add cranberry juice – do not stir, then serve.

WILD SCREW

29.1% alc/vol
2.1 standard drinks

30 ml (1 fl oz) Vodka
30 ml (1 fl oz) 101-Proof Wild Turkey Bourbon
30 ml (1 fl oz) Fresh Orange Juice

Pour ingredients into a cocktail shaker over ice and shake. Strain into a chilled cocktail glass and serve.

WHISKEY

Naughty Whiskey drinks include: *Slippery Surprise* – (don't we all love a surprise now and then), *Old Groaner* – (you're never too old), *Kiltlifter* – (what you see is what you get under there) and *Quickie* – (short and sweet).

Whiskey was invented by the Irish and not the Scots, as many people believe and that's not an Irish joke. Whiskey takes its name from the Irish meaning "water of life". Whiskey is a spirit that is distilled from a fermented mash of grain (usually barley, maize or rice) then aged in wooden barrels. There are five main categories: Irish Whiskey, Scotch Whisky, American Whiskey, Blended Whiskey and Rye Whiskey (Canadian).

Whiskey or Whisky – Only Irish and American Whiskies contain the 'e' in whiskey with the exception of Makers Mark Kentucky Straight Bourbon Whisky with the founder of the distillery being given permission to remove the 'e' due to his Scottish heritage

SLIPPERY SURPRISE

11% alc/vol
1.7 standard drinks

45 ml (1½ fl oz) Scotch Whisky
15 ml (½ fl oz) Banana Liqueur
60 ml (2 fl oz) Grapefruit Juice
60 ml (2 fl oz) Peach Juice
15 ml (½ fl oz) Passion-Fruit Juice
Slice of Orange
Strawberry

Pour Whisky, Liqueur and juices into a cocktail shaker over cracked ice. Shake and pour into a chilled goblet. Garnish with a slice of orange and a strawberry then serve.

SEXUAL HEALING

15.5% alc/vol
1.1 standard drinks

15 ml (½ fl oz) Bourbon
15 ml (½ fl oz) Amaretto
15 ml (½ fl oz) Sloe Gin
23 ml (¾ fl oz) Fresh Orange Juice
23 ml (¾ fl oz) Pineapple Juice

Pour ingredients into a cocktail shaker over ice and shake. Strain into a chilled old-fashioned glass and serve.

QUICKIE

39.1% alc/vol
3.1 standard drinks

45 ml (1½ fl oz) Bourbon
45 ml (1½ fl oz) Light Rum
10 ml (⅓ fl oz) Cointreau

Pour ingredients into a cocktail shaker over ice and shake. Strain into a chilled cocktail glass and serve.

TWIN PEAKS

34.4% alc/vol
1.8 standard drinks

45 ml (1½ fl oz) Blended Whiskey
15 ml (½ fl oz) Dubonnet
5 ml (⅙ fl oz) Cointreau
Wedge of Lemon

Pour Whiskey, Dubonnet and Cointreau into a mixing glass over ice. Stir and strain into a chilled cocktail glass. Garnish with a wedge of lemon and serve.

SEX ON THE RUG

22.5% alc/vol
4.3 standard drinks

90 ml (3 fl oz) Bourbon
90 ml (3 fl oz) Kahlúa
60 ml (2 fl oz) Fresh Milk (chilled)

Pour ingredients into a blender over crushed ice and blend. Pour into a chilled tall glass and serve with a straw.

IRISH HOOKER

34.1% alc/vol
1.3 standard drinks

30 ml (1 fl oz) Irish Whiskey
5 ml (⅙ fl oz) Bailey's Irish Cream
5 ml (⅙ fl oz) Frangelico
5 ml (⅙ fl oz) Irish Mist
5 ml (⅙ fl oz) Kahlúa

Pour ingredients into a cocktail shaker over ice and shake. Strain into an old-fashioned glass over ice and serve.

OLD GROANER

36% alc/vol
2.1 standard drinks

60 ml (2 fl oz) Canadian Whisky
15 ml (½ fl oz) Amaretto

Pour ingredients into an old-fashioned glass over ice, stir and serve.

TROUSER ROUSER

12.6% alc/vol
1.7 standard drinks

45 ml (1½ fl oz) Scotch Whisky
15 ml (½ fl oz) Banana Liqueur
60 ml (2 fl oz) Mango Juice
30 ml (1 fl oz) Pineapple Juice
15 ml (½ fl oz) Fresh Lime Juice
1 teaspoon Egg White
Maraschino Cherry
Sprig of Fresh Mint

Pour Whisky, Liqueur, juices and egg white into a cocktail shaker over ice. Shake and strain into a collins glass over cracked ice. Garnish with a cherry and sprig of mint then serve.

ERUPTION

34.4% alc/vol
2 standard drinks

60 ml (2 fl oz) Canadian Whisky
15 ml (½ fl oz) Crème De Cassis
Maraschino Cherry

Pour Whisky and Cassis into a mixing glass over ice.
Stir and strain into a chilled cocktail glass. Garnish
with a cherry and serve.

KILTLIFTER

20% alc/vol
2.4 standard drinks

45 ml (1½ fl oz) Scotch Whisky
30 ml (1 fl oz) Drambuie
75 ml (2½ fl oz) Fresh Lime Juice

Pour ingredients into a cocktail shaker over ice and
shake. Strain into an old-fashioned glass over ice
and serve.

CLIMAX
NO.2

28.5% alc/vol
2.4 standard drinks

60 ml (2 fl oz) Tennessee Whiskey
30 ml (1 fl oz) Kahlúa
15 ml (½ fl oz) Thick Cream

Pour ingredients into a cocktail shaker over ice and shake. Strain into a chilled cocktail glass and serve.

NIGHTIE
LIFTER

37% alc/vol
2.1 standard drinks

45 ml (1½ fl oz) Bourbon
23 ml (¾ fl oz) Blackberry Brandy
5 ml (⅙ fl oz) Peach Schnapps

Pour ingredients into a cocktail shaker over cracked ice and shake. Pour into a chilled old-fashioned glass and serve.

SPERM COUNT

12.7% alc/vol
2 standard drinks

45 ml (1½ fl oz) Scotch Whisky
30 ml (1 fl oz) Dark Crème De Cacao
120 ml (4 fl oz) Fresh Milk (chilled)

Pour ingredients into a cocktail shaker over cracked ice and shake. Pour into a chilled highball glass and serve.

UNDER THE KILT

27.2% alc/vol
1.6 standard drinks

30 ml (1 fl oz) Scotch Whisky
15 ml (½ fl oz) Banana Liqueur
15 ml (½ fl oz) Galliano
15 ml (½ fl oz) Fresh Cream
Dash of Fresh Lime Juice
2 Slices of Banana

Pour Whisky, Liqueur, Galliano, cream and juice into a cocktail shaker over ice. Shake and strain into a chilled cocktail glass. Garnish with slices of banana and serve.

GREATHEAD

38.5% alc/vol
1.8 standard drinks

45 ml (1½ fl oz) Canadian Whisky
15 ml (½ fl oz) Applejack

Pour ingredients into a mixing glass over ice and
stir. Strain into a chilled cocktail glass and serve.

TEQUILA

Naughty Tequila drinks include: *Turf Muncher* – (each to there own), *Golden Shower* – (might need a normal shower after) and *Wet Snatch* – (she's ready).

Tequila is a Mexican spirit distilled from the blue agave plant which is also known as the century plant. This plant resembles a large pineapple with spikes similar to the cactus plant, growing in abundance in the desert.

There are two varieties of Tequila; White or Silver and Gold. White Tequila is aged for a very short period of time in wax-lined vats. Gold Tequila is aged in Whisky barrels for usually between two and four years until the spirit changes to a golden color and is then ready to be bottled.

BIG RED HOOTER

8.8% alc/vol
1.4 standard drinks

30 ml (1 fl oz) Tequila
23 ml (¾ fl oz) Amaretto
30 ml (1 fl oz) Grenadine
120 ml (4 fl oz) Pineapple Juice
Maraschino Cherry

Pour Tequila and Amaretto into a collins glass over ice then stir. Add juice and stir again. Add Grenadine by pouring on top of drink – do not stir, then garnish with a cherry and serve with a straw.

TURF MUNCHER

9.8% alc/vol
1.4 standard drinks

30 ml (1 fl oz) Tequila
30 ml (1 fl oz) Midori
120 ml (4 fl oz) Grapefruit Juice
Maraschino Cherry

Pour Tequila and juice into a cocktail shaker over cracked ice. Shake and pour into a chilled highball glass. Add Midori by pouring into centre of drink – do not stir, then garnish with a cherry and serve.

SILK STOCKINGS

19.8% alc/vol
1.9 standard drinks

45 ml (1½ fl oz) Tequila
30 ml (1 fl oz) White Crème De Cacao
Dash of Grenadine
45 ml (1½ fl oz) Fresh Cream
Maraschino Cherry
Cinnamon

Pour Tequila, Cacao, Grenadine and cream into a cocktail shaker over ice. Shake and strain into a chilled cocktail glass. Sprinkle cinnamon on top and garnish with a cherry then serve.

HOT PANTS

26.8% alc/vol
1.6 standard drinks

45 ml (1½ fl oz) Tequila
15 ml (½ fl oz) Peppermint Schnapps
10 ml (⅓ fl oz) Grapefruit Juice
1 teaspoon Sugar Syrup

Prepare an old-fashioned glass with a salt frosted rim. Pour ingredients into a cocktail shaker over cracked ice and shake. Pour into prepared glass and serve.

BUTTOCK CLENCHER

12.9% alc/vol
1.9 standard drinks

30 ml (1 fl oz) Tequila
30 ml (1 fl oz) Dry Gin
8 ml (¼ fl oz) Midori
60 ml (2 fl oz) Pineapple Juice
60 ml (2 fl oz) Lemonade
Maraschino Cherry
Slice of Pineapple

Pour Tequila, Gin, Midori and juice into a cocktail shaker over ice. Shake and strain into a highball glass over ice. Add lemonade and stir gently. Garnish with a cherry and a slice of pineapple then serve.

GOLDEN SHOWER

37.4% alc/vol
2.2 standard drinks

60 ml (2 fl oz) Tequila
15 ml (½ fl oz) Galliano

Pour ingredients into a mixing glass over ice and stir. Strain into a chilled cocktail glass and serve.

HORNY BULL

9.5% alc/vol
1.3 standard drinks

45 ml (1½ fl oz) Tequila
15 ml (½ fl oz) Grenadine
90 ml (3 fl oz) Fresh Orange Juice
30 ml (1 fl oz) Lemonade
Cherry
Wedge of Orange

Pour Tequila, Grenadine and juice into a blender over crushed ice. Blend and pour into a chilled margarita glass. Add lemonade and stir gently. Garnish with a cherry and wedge of orange then serve.

SCRATCH AND SNIFF

10.9% alc/vol
1.5 standard drinks

45 ml (1½ fl oz) Tequila
15 ml (½ fl oz) Chambord
60 ml (2 fl oz) Fresh Orange Juice
60 ml (2 fl oz) Pineapple Juice

Pour ingredients into a cocktail shaker over ice and shake. Strain into a highball glass half filled with ice and serve.

WET SNATCH

12.7% alc/vol
1.8 standard drinks

60 ml (2 fl oz) Tequila
40 ml (1 fl oz) Pineapple Juice
40 ml (1 fl oz) Coconut Milk (chilled)
20 ml (⅔ fl oz) Raspberry Juice
20 ml (⅔ fl oz) Vanilla Syrup
Fresh Whipped Cream

Pour juices, milk and syrup into a blender over cracked ice. Blend well then add Tequila and blend again. Pour into a chilled highball glass, float cream on top and serve.

SHOOTERS

Naughty Shooter drinks include: *G-Spot* – (stay focused), *Vibrator* – (BOB – battery operated boyfriend), *Stained Blue Dress* – (remember Bill and Monica?), *Tired Pussy* – (been a long hard night) and *Sex in the Snow* – (good way to melt snow).

Shooters originated in America where liquors such as Scotch Whisky or Bourbon were served in shot glasses, with other liqueurs added and should be swallowed in one gulp.

You can have a lot of fun with shots at parties but be mindful that if you have too many then you will not be feeling too good!

The ingredients of each drink are required to be layered in the order given to create a layered effect. The ingredients for some shooters are shaken or stirred over ice and then poured into the selected glass to be served as a shooter or shot.

SEX IN THE PARKING LOT

24.5% alc/vol
0.9 standard drinks

15 ml (½ fl oz) Apple Schnapps
15 ml (½ fl oz) Chambord
15 ml (½ fl oz) Vodka

Pour ingredients into a cocktail shaker over ice and shake. Strain into a chilled shot glass and serve.

BLOW JOB

15.7% alc/vol
0.6 standard drinks

15 ml (½ fl oz) Kahlúa
10 ml (⅓ fl oz) Banana Liqueur
15 ml (½ fl oz) Bailey's Irish Cream
Fresh Whipped Cream

Layer ingredients in order given into a tall Dutch cordial glass, float cream on top and serve.

SWEET TITS

19.7% alc/vol
0.5 standard drinks

15 ml (½ fl oz) Apricot Brandy
15 ml (½ fl oz) Strawberry Liqueur
5 ml (⅙ fl oz) Pineapple Juice

Pour ingredients into a cocktail shaker over ice and shake. Strain into a chilled shot glass and serve.

FLAMING ORGY

25.8% alc/vol
0.9 standard drinks

10 ml (⅓ fl oz) Grenadine
10 ml (⅓ fl oz) Green Crème De Menthe
15 ml (½ fl oz) Brandy
10 ml (⅓ fl oz) Tequila

Layer ingredients in order given into a tall Dutch cordial glass and serve.

LEG SPREADER

32.3% alc/vol
1.2 standard drinks

23 ml (¾ fl oz) Sambuca
23 ml (¾ fl oz) Tia Maria

Layer ingredients in order given into a shot glass and serve.

HARD ON

16% alc/vol
0.4 standard drinks

10 ml (⅓ fl oz) Kahlúa
10 ml (⅓ fl oz) Amaretto
10 ml (⅓ fl oz) Fresh Cream

Layer ingredients in order given into a cordial Lexington glass and serve.

AGGRESSIVE BLOWJOB

23.8% alc/vol
0.8 standard drinks

10 ml (⅓ fl oz) Everclear
30 ml (1 fl oz) Cola

Pour Everclear into a shot glass and add cola, stir gently then serve.

JUICY PUSSY

12.4% alc/vol
0.4 standard drinks

15 ml (½ fl oz) Bailey's Irish Cream
15 ml (½ fl oz) Peach Schnapps
15 ml (½ fl oz) Pineapple Juice

Pour ingredients into a cocktail shaker over ice and shake. Strain into a chilled shot glass and serve.

69ER

26.1% alc/vol
0.9 standard drinks

15 ml (½ fl oz) Banana Liqueur
15 ml (½ fl oz) Bailey's Irish Cream
15 ml (½ fl oz) Ouzo

Layer ingredients in order given into a shot glass and serve.

SEX ON THE BEACH SHOOTER

12.5% alc/vol
0.3 standard drinks

10 ml (⅓ fl oz) Chambord
10 ml (⅓ fl oz) Midori
10 ml (⅓ fl oz) Pineapple Juice

Pour ingredients into a cocktail shaker over ice and shake. Strain into a chilled shot glass and serve.

Q.F.

19.7% alc/vol
0.5 standard drinks

12 ml (⅖ fl oz) Kahlúa
12 ml (⅖ fl oz) Midori
8 ml (¼ fl oz) Bailey's Irish Cream

Layer ingredients in order given into a cordial Embassy glass and serve.

CHASTITY BELT

20.2% alc/vol
0.6 standard drinks

15 ml (½ fl oz) Tia Maria
10 ml (⅓ fl oz) Frangelico
10 ml (⅓ fl oz) Bailey's Irish Cream
5 ml (⅙ fl oz) Fresh Cream

Layer ingredients in order given into a tall Dutch cordial glass and serve.

LICK IT REAL GOOD

19% alc/vol
0.7 standard drinks

23 ml (¾ fl oz) Tequila
23 ml (¾ fl oz) Fresh Orange Juice

Pour ingredients into a shot glass, stir and serve.

DEEP THROAT

24% alc/vol
0.9 standard drinks

20 ml (⅔ fl oz) Kahlúa
20 ml (⅔ fl oz) Grand Marnier
Fresh Whipped Cream

Layer ingredients in order given into a tall Dutch cordial glass, float cream on top and serve.

ORGASM SHOOTER

28.5% alc/vol
1 standard drink

23 ml (¾ fl oz) Cointreau
23 ml (¾ fl oz) Bailey's Irish Cream

Layer ingredients in order given into a shot glass and serve.

G-SPOT

17.8% alc/vol
0.6 standard drinks

15 ml (½ fl oz) Chambord
15 ml (½ fl oz) Southern Comfort
15 ml (½ fl oz) Fresh Orange Juice

Pour ingredients into a cocktail shaker over ice and shake. Strain into a chilled shot glass and serve.

VIBRATOR

30.4% alc/vol
0.7 standard drinks

10 ml (⅓ fl oz) Bailey's Irish Cream
20 ml (⅔ fl oz) Southern Comfort

Layer ingredients in order given into a cordial Embassy glass and serve.

BLOW ME

20.7% alc/vol
0.6 standard drinks

10 ml (⅓ fl oz) Kahlúa
15 ml (½ fl oz) Midori
10 ml (⅓ fl oz) Malibu

Layer ingredients in order given into a cordial Embassy glass and serve.
This drink was created by the author of this book.

JENNIFER'S ORGASM

27.5% alc/vol
0.9 standard drinks

20 ml (⅔ fl oz) Butterscotch Schnapps
20 ml (⅔ fl oz) Spiced Rum

Pour ingredients into a cocktail shaker over ice and shake. Strain into a chilled shot glass and serve.

SOUTHERN BONDAGE

20.9% alc/vol
0.7 standard drinks

8 ml (¼ fl oz) Southern Comfort
8 ml (¼ fl oz) Amaretto
8 ml (¼ fl oz) Peach Schnapps
8 ml (¼ fl oz) Triple Sec
5 ml (⅙ fl oz) Cranberry Juice
5 ml (⅙ fl oz) Sweet and Sour Mix

Pour ingredients into a cocktail shaker over ice and shake. Strain into a chilled shot glass and serve.

SOUR PUSSY

40.8% alc/vol
1.1 standard drinks

15 ml (½ fl oz) Everclear
5 ml (⅙ fl oz) Grenadine
15 ml (½ fl oz) Fresh Lemon Juice

Pour ingredients into a shot glass, stir and serve.

COCK SUCKING COWBOY

19.5% alc/vol
0.5 standard drinks

30 ml (1 fl oz) Butterscotch Schnapps
5 ml (⅙ fl oz) Bailey's Irish Cream

Layer ingredients in order given into a shot glass and serve.

STAINED BLUE DRESS

31% alc/vol
0.7 standard drinks

15 ml (½ fl oz) Vodka
15 ml (½ fl oz) Blue Curaçao
2 drops Bailey's Irish Cream

Pour Vodka into a cordial Embassy glass and layer Curaçao on top. Add Bailey's by drops and serve.

RUG-MUNCHER

18.5% alc/vol
0.6 standard drinks

20 ml (⅔ fl oz) Bailey's Irish Cream
20 ml (⅔ fl oz) Root Beer Schnapps

Pour ingredients into a cocktail shaker over ice and shake. Strain into a chilled shot glass and serve.

NYMPHO- MANIAC

27.8% alc/vol
1.3 standard drinks

30 ml (1 fl oz) Spiced Rum
15 ml (½ fl oz) Malibu
15 ml (½ fl oz) Peach Schnapps

Pour ingredients into a cocktail shaker over ice and shake. Strain into a chilled large shot glass and serve.

DIRTY NIPPLE

27.5% alc/vol
0.9 standard drinks

20 ml (⅔ fl oz) Sambuca
20 ml (⅔ fl oz) Bailey's Irish Cream

Layer ingredients in order given into a cordial Lexington glass and serve.

SEX IN THE SNOW

28% alc/vol
0.8 standard drinks

12 ml (⅖ fl oz) Triple Sec
12 ml (⅖ fl oz) Malibu
12 ml (⅖ fl oz) Ouzo

Layer ingredients in order given into a cordial Lexington glass, stir gently and shoot through a straw.

TIRED PUSSY

18.1% alc/vol
0.6 standard drinks

38 ml (1¼ fl oz) Malibu
3 dashes Cranberry Juice
3 dashes Pineapple Juice

Pour ingredients into a cocktail shaker over ice and shake. Strain into a chilled shot glass and serve.

WHITE MESS

19.7% alc/vol
0.6 standard drinks

8 ml (¼ fl oz) Bacardi
8 ml (¼ fl oz) Crème De Cassis
8 ml (¼ fl oz) Malibu
8 ml (¼ fl oz) Root Beer Schnapps
8 ml (¼ fl oz) Thick Cream

Pour ingredients into a cocktail shaker over ice and shake. Strain into a chilled shot glass and serve.

SPERM SHOT

11.5% alc/vol
0.3 standard drinks

15 ml (½ fl oz) Banana Liqueur
15 ml (½ fl oz) Fresh Cream

Pour ingredients into a shot glass, stir and serve.

69ER IN A POOL

54.4% alc/vol
1.3 standard drinks

15 ml (½ fl oz) Vodka
Dash of Fresh Lemon Juice
15 ml (½ fl oz) 151-Proof Bacardi
Drop of Tabasco Sauce

Layer ingredients in order given into a shot glass and serve.

SLIPPERY NIPPLE

31% alc/vol
1.1 standard drinks

30 ml (1 fl oz) Sambuca
15 ml (½ fl oz) Bailey's Irish Cream

Layer ingredients in order given into a tall Dutch cordial glass and serve.

SWELL SEX

20.7% alc/vol
0.6 standard drinks

10 ml (⅓ fl oz) Malibu
10 ml (⅓ fl oz) Midori
10 ml (⅓ fl oz) Vodka
5 ml (⅙ fl oz) Pineapple Juice
½ teaspoon Fresh Cream

Pour ingredients into a cocktail shaker over ice and shake. Strain into a chilled shot glass and serve.

HORNY GIRLSCOUT

20% alc/vol
0.5 standard drinks

15 ml (½ fl oz) Kahlúa
15 ml (½ fl oz) Peppermint Schnapps

Layer ingredients in order given into a cordial Embassy glass and serve.

FU2

19.2% alc/vol
0.5 standard drinks

10 ml (⅓ fl oz) Kahlúa
5 ml (⅙ fl oz) Frangelico
15 ml (½ fl oz) Bailey's Irish Cream

Layer ingredients in order given into a cordial
Embassy glass and serve.
This drink was created by the author of this book.

DIRTY ORGASM

30.7% alc/vol
1.1 standard drinks

15 ml (½ fl oz) Cointreau
15 ml (½ fl oz) Galliano
15 ml (½ fl oz) Bailey's Irish Cream

Layer ingredients in order given into a tall Dutch
cordial glass and serve.

SOUTHERN COMFORT

Naughty Southern Comfort drinks include: *Slow and Comfortable Screw* – (Just want a relaxing fun time), *Eight Inch Tongue* – (a girls dream), *Sex on My Face* – (what you could do with that Eight Inch Tongue) and *Climax* – (ultimate goal of both).

Southern Comfort originated in the late 19th century in the south of America where peaches were marinated in Bourbon, this drink was known as Cuffs and Buttons. The drink became so popular that a distiller named M.W. Heron perfected Southern Comfort, creating a sweet smooth Bourbon-based peach liqueur as we know it today. I wonder what he would think of the names of drinks that his Southern Comfort is used in today!

SLOW COMFORTABLE SCREW IN BETWEEN THE SHEETS

9.8% alc/vol
1.6 standard drinks

15 ml (½ fl oz) Southern Comfort
15 ml (½ fl oz) Vodka
15 ml (½ fl oz) Cointreau
15 ml (½ fl oz) Sloe Gin
150 ml (5 fl oz) Fresh Orange Juice

Build ingredients into a collins glass over ice then serve with a swizzle stick and straw.

COMFORTABLE SCREW UP AGAINST A WALL

13.8% alc/vol
1.6 standard drinks

23 ml (¾ fl oz) Southern Comfort
23 ml (¾ fl oz) Vodka
8 ml (¼ fl oz) Galliano
90 ml (3 fl oz) Fresh Orange Juice

Pour ingredients into a cocktail shaker over ice and shake. Strain into a highball glass half filled with ice and serve.

SLOW AND COMFORTABLE SCREW

18.5% alc/vol
2.6 standard drinks

30 ml (1 fl oz) Southern Comfort
30 ml (1 fl oz) Dry Gin
30 ml (1 fl oz) Vodka
90 ml (3 fl oz) Fresh Orange Juice
Slice of Orange

Pour Southern Comfort, Gin and Vodka into a mixing glass over ice. Stir and strain into a highball glass over ice. Add juice and stir. Garnish with a slice of orange and serve.

SLOW COMFORT SCREW

9% alc/vol
1.5 standard drinks

30 ml (1 fl oz) Southern Comfort
30 ml (1 fl oz) Sloe Gin
150 ml (5 fl oz) Fresh Orange Juice
Slice of Orange

Pour Southern Comfort and Gin into a cocktail shaker over ice. Shake and strain into a highball glass over ice. Add juice and stir. Garnish with a slice of orange and serve.

EIGHT INCH TONGUE

22.8% alc/vol
1.9 standard drinks

15 ml (½ fl oz) Southern Comfort
15 ml (½ fl oz) Amaretto
15 ml (½ fl oz) Brandy
15 ml (½ fl oz) Peach Schnapps
15 ml (½ fl oz) Vodka
30 ml (1 fl oz) Cranberry Juice

Pour ingredients into a mixing glass over ice and stir. Strain into a chilled highball glass and serve.

SLOW COMFORTABLE SCREW ON A DOGBOX

17.8% alc/vol
3.7 standard drinks

45 ml (1½ fl oz) Southern Comfort
45 ml (1½ fl oz) Sloe Gin
45 ml (1½ fl oz) Tennessee Whiskey
5 ml (⅙ fl oz) Grenadine
120 ml (4 fl oz) Fresh Orange Juice

Pour ingredients into a cocktail shaker over ice and shake. Strain into a collins glass over ice and serve.

SLOW COMFORTABLE SCREW – MEXICAN STYLE

9.6% alc/vol
1.6 standard drinks

15 ml (½ fl oz) Southern Comfort
15 ml (½ fl oz) Sloe Gin
15 ml (½ fl oz) Galliano
15 ml (½ fl oz) Tequila
150 ml (5 fl oz) Fresh Orange Juice

Build ingredients into a collins glass over ice then serve with a swizzle stick and straw.

COMFORTABLE SCREW

10.1% alc/vol
1.3 standard drinks

30 ml (1 fl oz) Southern Comfort
15 ml (½ fl oz) Vodka
120 ml (4 fl oz) Fresh Orange Juice
Slice of Orange

Pour Southern Comfort and Vodka into an old-fashioned glass over ice then stir. Add juice and stir well. Garnish with a slice of orange and serve.

SEX ON MY FACE

26.2% alc/vol
1.6 standard drinks

15 ml (½ fl oz) Southern Comfort
15 ml (½ fl oz) Banana Liqueur
15 ml (½ fl oz) Malibu
15 ml (½ fl oz) Yukon Jack
5 ml (⅙ fl oz) Cranberry Juice
5 ml (⅙ fl oz) Fresh Orange Juice
5 ml (⅙ fl oz) Pineapple Juice

Pour ingredients into a tall glass filled with ice, stir well and serve.

CLIMAX

21.6% alc/vol
1.8 standard drinks

45 ml (1½ fl oz) Southern Comfort
30 ml (1 fl oz) Kahlúa
30 ml (1 fl oz) Whipping Cream

Pour ingredients into a cocktail shaker over cracked ice and shake. Pour into a chilled old-fashioned glass and serve.

COMFORTABLE FUZZY SCREW

16.6% alc/vol
3.3 standard drinks

45 ml (1½ fl oz) Southern Comfort
45 ml (1½ fl oz) Peach Schnapps
45 ml (1½ fl oz) Vodka
120 ml (4 fl oz) Fresh Orange Juice
Slice of Orange

Pour Southern Comfort, Schnapps and Vodka into a mixing glass over ice. Stir and strain into a highball glass over ice. Add juice and stir. Garnish with a slice of orange and serve.

VELVET TONGUE

15% alc/vol
2.7 standard drinks

45 ml (1½ fl oz) Southern Comfort
45 ml (1½ fl oz) Canadian Whisky
135 ml (4½ fl oz) Dry Ginger Ale

Pour Southern Comfort and Whisky into a mixing glass over ice. Stir and strain into a highball glass over ice. Add ginger ale, stir gently and serve.

SHAG IN THE SAND

16.8% alc/vol
3.4 standard drinks

50 ml (1 fl oz) Southern Comfort
50 ml (1 fl oz) Sloe Gin
20 ml (⅔ fl oz) Vodka
15 ml (½ fl oz) Red Curaçao
20 ml (⅔ fl oz) Grenadine
100 ml (3 fl oz) Fresh Orange Juice

Pour ingredients into a cocktail shaker over ice and shake. Strain into a collins glass over ice and serve.

BAILEY'S IRISH CREAM

Naughty Bailey's drinks include: *Screaming Orgasm* – (letting the neighbours know what you're up to), *Wet Pussy* – (nice and warm), *Multiple Orgasm* – (if only guys had that ability) and *Sex Machine* – (make sure batteries are charged).

Bailey's Original Irish Cream liqueur is a product of the Republic of Ireland produced from fine Irish Whiskey and blended with smooth Irish cream, creating a creamy chocolate flavor liqueur with the hint of Whiskey that was created in 1974. The Irish sure got this one right.

SCREAMING ORGASM

20.5% alc/vol
1.9 standard drinks

30 ml (1 fl oz) Bailey's Irish Cream
30 ml (1 fl oz) Galliano
15 ml (½ fl oz) Cointreau
15 ml (½ fl oz) Kahlúa
30 ml (1 fl oz) Fresh Cream

Pour ingredients into a cocktail shaker over ice and shake. Strain into a chilled cocktail glass and serve.

DIRTY PANTY

23.3% alc/vol
0.6 standard drinks

8 ml (¼ fl oz) Bailey's Irish Cream
8 ml (¼ fl oz) Sambuca
8 ml (¼ fl oz) Tequila
1½ teaspoons Tabasco Sauce
Parmesan Cheese

Pour Bailey's, Sambuca, Tequila and sauce into a mixing glass over ice. Stir and strain into a chilled cocktail glass. Sprinkle parmesan on top and serve.

SHUDDERING ORGASM

21.7% alc/vol
1.5 standard drinks

30 ml (1 fl oz) Bailey's Irish Cream
30 ml (1 fl oz) Amaretto
30 ml (1 fl oz) Kahlúa

Pour ingredients into a cocktail shaker over ice and shake. Strain into a chilled cocktail glass and serve.

KINKY ORGASM

4.9% alc/vol
1 standard drink

20 ml (⅔ fl oz) Bailey's Irish Cream
20 ml (⅔ fl oz) Amaretto
20 ml (⅔ fl oz) Kahlúa
210 ml (7 fl oz) Fresh Milk (chilled)
2 Strawberries

Pour Bailey's, Amaretto, Kahlúa and milk into a chilled highball glass then stir well. Add strawberries and serve.

CARESSER

9.1% alc/vol
1.3 standard drinks

30 ml (1 fl oz) Bailey's Irish Cream
30 ml (1 fl oz) Bacardi
120 ml (4 fl oz) Fresh Milk (chilled)

Pour ingredients into a highball glass over ice, stir and serve.

CREAMY ORGASM

16.4% alc/vol
1.4 standard drinks

30 ml (1 fl oz) Bailey's Irish Cream
30 ml (1 fl oz) Cointreau
45 ml (1½ fl oz) Thick Cream
Strawberry

Pour Bailey's, Cointreau and cream into a cocktail shaker over ice. Shake and strain into a chilled brandy balloon. Garnish with a strawberry and serve.

SCREAMING ORGASM NO.2

30.7% alc/vol
3.3 standard drinks

45 ml (1½ fl oz) Bailey's Irish Cream
45 ml (1½ fl oz) Cointreau
45 ml (1½ fl oz) Galliano

Pour ingredients into a cocktail shaker over ice and shake. Strain into a chilled highball glass and serve.

ORGASMIC FANTASY

21.8% alc/vol
1.7 standard drinks

45 ml (1½ fl oz) Bailey's Irish Cream
30 ml (1 fl oz) Vodka
15 ml (½ fl oz) Kahlúa
2 teaspoons Vanilla Extract

Pour ingredients into a cocktail glass over crushed ice, stir and serve.

MULTIPLE ORGASM

28.4% alc/vol
1.7 standard drinks

30 ml (1 fl oz) Bailey's Irish Cream
30 ml (1 fl oz) Cointreau
15 ml (½ fl oz) Amaretto

Pour ingredients into a cocktail glass over cracked ice, stir and serve.

DIRTY GIRL SCOUT

24.6% alc/vol
1.8 standard drinks

30 ml (1 fl oz) Bailey's Irish Cream
30 ml (1 fl oz) Kahlúa
30 ml (1 fl oz) Vodka
5 ml (⅙ fl oz) Green Crème De Menthe

Pour ingredients into a cocktail shaker over ice and shake. Strain into an old-fashioned glass over ice and serve.

ORGASM

28.5% alc/vol
1.3 standard drinks

30 ml (1 fl oz) Bailey's Irish Cream
30 ml (1 fl oz) Cointreau

Pour ingredients into a brandy balloon over ice, stir and serve.

CREAMY KISS

16.3% alc/vol
1.5 standard drinks

30 ml (1 fl oz) Bailey's Irish Cream
30 ml (1 fl oz) Amaretto
30 ml (1 fl oz) Peach Schnapps
30 ml (1 fl oz) Fresh Cream

Pour ingredients into a highball glass over ice, stir and serve.

WET PUSSY

5.6% alc/vol
1.2 standard drinks

60 ml (2 fl oz) Bailey's Irish Cream
30 ml (1 fl oz) Chambord
180 ml (6 fl oz) Fresh Milk (chilled)

Pour ingredients into a cocktail shaker over ice and shake. Strain into a chilled highball glass and serve.

SEX MACHINE

12.4% alc/vol
1.3 standard drinks

45 ml (1½ fl oz) Bailey's Irish Cream
45 ml (1½ fl oz) Kahlúa
45 ml (1½ fl oz) Fresh Milk (chilled)

Pour ingredients into a cocktail shaker over cracked ice and shake. Pour into a chilled old-fashioned glass and serve.

TONGUE TANGLER

7.9% alc/vol
0.8 standard drinks

30 ml (1 fl oz) Bailey's Irish Cream
15 ml (½ fl oz) Brandy
90 ml (3 fl oz) Thick Cream

Pour ingredients into a chilled old-fashioned glass over a few ice cubes, stir well and serve.

SCREAMING ORGASM NO.3

25.7% alc/vol
2.7 standard drinks

45 ml (1½ fl oz) Bailey's Irish Cream
45 ml (1½ fl oz) Peachtree
45 ml (1½ fl oz) Vodka

Pour ingredients into a cocktail shaker over ice and shake. Strain into a chilled highball glass and serve.

FROZEN ORGASM

11.5% alc/vol
1.3 standard drinks

This drink is an Orgasm (page 136) that is blended over crushed ice, served in a chilled margarita glass and garnished with a strawberry.

MIDORI

Naughty Midori drinks include: *Skinny Dipper* – (feeling free while cooling off), *Wet Spot* – (Turned on and ready), *Bald Pussy* – (smooth as silk) and *Sex in a Tree* – (watch out for those splinters).

Midori is a light refreshing honeydew melon-flavor liqueur produced by Suntory Limited in Japan. First launched in the United States in 1978, Midori is a great additive in long cool drinks to cool down after becoming over heated with passionate activities.

ISLAND AFFAIR

8.3% alc/vol
1.3 standard drinks

38 ml (1¼ fl oz) Midori
15 ml (½ fl oz) Cointreau
15 ml (½ fl oz) Blue Curaçao
60 ml (2 fl oz) Mango Juice
45 ml (1½ fl oz) Fresh Orange Juice
Fresh Whipped Cream
Cherry
Slice of Orange

Pour Midori, Cointreau and juices into a cocktail shaker over ice. Shake and strain into a hurricane glass over cracked ice. Add Curaçao – do not stir, then float cream on top. Garnish with a cherry and slice of orange then serve with 2 straws.

SEDUCTION

19.4% alc/vol
1.4 standard drinks

30 ml (1 fl oz) Midori
30 ml (1 fl oz) Kahlúa
30 ml (1 fl oz) Bailey's Irish Cream

Build ingredients into an old-fashioned glass over ice and serve with a swizzle stick.

WET SPOT

7.9% alc/vol
0.8 standard drinks

30 ml (1 fl oz) Midori
15 ml (½ fl oz) Frangelico
30 ml (1 fl oz) Apple Juice
30 ml (1 fl oz) Fresh Cream
Pulp of 1 Passion-Fruit
Cherry
Slice of Pineapple

Pour Midori, Frangelico, juice and cream into a cocktail shaker over ice. Shake and strain into a chilled cocktail glass then layer passion-fruit on top. Garnish with a cherry and slice of pineapple then serve.

SKINNY DIPPER

5.3% alc/vol
1 standard drink

60 ml (2 fl oz) Midori
180 ml (6 fl oz) Cranberry Juice

Pour ingredients into a mixing glass over ice and stir. Strain into a tall glass over ice and serve.

BALD PUSSY

25.4% alc/vol
3.8 standard drinks

45 ml (1½ fl oz) Midori
45 ml (1½ fl oz) Blueberry Schnapps
30 ml (1 fl oz) Citrus Vodka
30 ml (1 fl oz) Triple Sec
30 ml (1 fl oz) Vodka
5 ml (⅙ fl oz) Fresh Lime Juice
5 ml (⅙ fl oz) Lemon-Lime Soda

Pour Midori, Schnapps, Vodkas, Triple Sec and juice into a cocktail shaker over cracked ice. Shake and pour into a chilled highball glass. Add soda – do not stir, then serve.

LEG-SPREADER

6% alc/vol
1.3 standard drinks

38 ml (1¼ fl oz) Midori
38 ml (1¼ fl oz) Malibu
180 ml (6 fl oz) Pineapple Juice
10 ml (⅓ fl oz) Lemonade

Pour Midori, Malibu and juice into a tall glass over ice then stir. Add lemonade, stir gently and serve.

MARTIAN SEX MONSTER

19.5% alc/vol
1.9 standard drinks

30 ml (1 fl oz) Midori
23 ml (¾ fl oz) Cognac
23 ml (¾ fl oz) Galliano
1½ scoops Vanilla Ice Cream

Pour Cognac and Galliano into a blender over a small amount of crushed ice then add ice cream. Blend and pour into a chilled highball glass. Layer Midori on top and serve with 2 straws.

SEX IN A TREE

9.8% alc/vol
1.7 standard drinks

38 ml (1¼ fl oz) Midori
30 ml (1 fl oz) Banana Liqueur
30 ml (1 fl oz) Malibu
120 ml (4 fl oz) Pineapple Juice

Pour ingredients into a tall glass half filled with ice, stir well and serve.

RANDY LITTLE KIWI

14.1% alc/vol
1.4 standard drinks

30 ml (1 fl oz) Midori
30 ml (1 fl oz) Vodka
½ teaspoon Sugar Syrup
1 Fresh Kiwi Fruit (sliced)

Pour sugar into a cocktail shaker and add sliced kiwi fruit then muddle well. Add ice, Midori and Vodka. Shake and strain into a brandy balloon over ice then serve.

JUNGLE LUST

8.3% alc/vol
1.4 standard drinks

30 ml (1 fl oz) Midori
30 ml (1 fl oz) Vodka
60 ml (2 fl oz) Fresh Orange Juice
60 ml (2 fl oz) Pineapple Juice
30 ml (1 fl oz) Peach Nectar

Pour ingredients into a cocktail shaker over ice and shake. Strain into a highball glass over ice and serve.

SEX UNDER THE BOARDWALK

19.2% alc/vol
1.4 standard drinks

30 ml (1 fl oz) Midori
30 ml (1 fl oz) Chambord
30 ml (1 fl oz) Peach Schnapps

Pour ingredients into a cocktail shaker over ice and shake. Strain into a chilled old-fashioned glass and serve.

FUZZY BALLS

8.6% alc/vol
0.9 standard drinks

15 ml (½ fl oz) Midori
15 ml (½ fl oz) Peach Schnapps
15 ml (½ fl oz) Vodka
45 ml (1½ fl oz) Cranberry Juice
45 ml (1½ fl oz) Grapefruit Juice

Pour ingredients into a mixing glass over ice and stir. Strain into a chilled old-fashioned glass and serve.

TROPICAL
SEX

4.2% alc/vol
1 standard drink

30 ml (1 fl oz) Midori
30 ml (1 fl oz) Malibu
240 ml (8 fl oz) Pineapple Juice
Slice of Kiwi Fruit

Pour Midori, Malibu and juice into a blender over cracked ice. Blend and pour into a chilled hurricane glass. Garnish with a slice of kiwi fruit and serve.

RUSTY
NUTS

11.3% alc/vol
2.7 standard drinks

90 ml (3 fl oz) Midori
60 ml (2 fl oz) Red Curaçao
150 ml (5 fl oz) Soda Water

Pour Midori and Curaçao into a mixing glass over ice. Stir and strain into a chilled highball glass. Add soda, stir gently and serve.

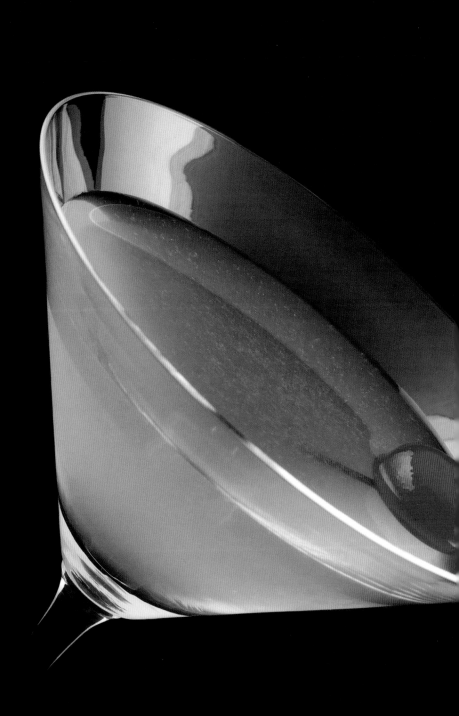

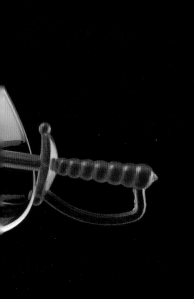

COINTREAU

Naughty Cointreau drinks include: *Hot Dream* – (then reality kicks in), *Between the Sheets* – (anything goes) and *Crazy Orgasm* – (uncontrollable wetness).

Cointreau is a clear orange-flavor liqueur created in 1849 by Adolphe Cointreau and his brother Edouard-Jean in Angers, France.

Tropical sweet and bitter orange peels are distilled to create Cointreau from a secret recipe that has been passed down through the generations of the Cointreau family.

DANGEROUS LIAISONS

26.6% alc/vol
1.6 standard drinks

30 ml (1 fl oz) Cointreau
30 ml (1 fl oz) Tia Maria
15 ml (½ fl oz) Sweet and Sour Mix

Pour ingredients into a cocktail shaker over ice and shake. Strain into a chilled sherry glass and serve.

HOT DREAM

16.4% alc/vol
1.4 standard drinks

30 ml (1 fl oz) Cointreau
15 ml (½ fl oz) Galliano
30 ml (1 fl oz) Pineapple Juice
30 ml (1 fl oz) Fresh Cream

Pour ingredients into a cocktail shaker over ice and shake. Strain into a chilled champagne saucer and serve.

BETWEEN THE SHEETS

28.8% alc/vol
1.4 standard drinks

15 ml (½ fl oz) Cointreau
15 ml (½ fl oz) Brandy
15 ml (½ fl oz) Light Rum
15 ml (½ fl oz) Fresh Lemon Juice

Pour ingredients into a cocktail shaker over ice and shake. Strain into a chilled cocktail glass and serve.

BURNING DESIRE

17.1% alc/vol
1.4 standard drinks

30 ml (1 fl oz) Cointreau
15 ml (½ fl oz) Galliano
5 ml (⅙ fl oz) Grenadine
50 ml (1 fl oz) Fresh Orange Juice
Dash of Egg White

Pour ingredients into a cocktail shaker over ice and shake. Strain into a chilled champagne saucer and serve.

TIGHT LIPS

30.8% alc/vol
1.8 standard drinks

30 ml (1 fl oz) Cointreau
30 ml (1 fl oz) Bacardi
15 ml (½ fl oz) Grenadine
Dash of Egg White

Pour ingredients into a cocktail shaker over ice and shake. Strain into a chilled cocktail glass and serve.

ORGASM NO.2

21.4% alc/vol
1.5 standard drinks

15 ml (½ fl oz) Cointreau
15 ml (½ fl oz) Amaretto
15 ml (½ fl oz) Vodka
15 ml (½ fl oz) White Crème De Cacao
30 ml (1 fl oz) Fresh Cream

Pour ingredients into a cocktail shaker over ice and shake. Strain into a chilled cocktail glass and serve.

CRAZY ORGASM

10% alc/vol
1.8 standard drinks

30 ml (1 fl oz) Cointreau
30 ml (1 fl oz) Vodka
83 ml (2¾ fl oz) Cranberry Juice
83 ml (2¾ fl oz) Fresh Orange Juice
1 teaspoon Sugar Syrup

Pour ingredients into a tall glass over ice, stir well and serve.

SCHNAPPS

Naughty Schnapps drinks include: *Sex in the Shower* – (who's going down... to pick up the soap), *Affair* – (Don't get caught), *A Boner* – (he's ready for you) and *Red Headed Slut* – (gotta watch out for the red heads).

Schnapps is a German word and is the generic term for white (clear) Brandies that are distilled from fruits.

Traditional Schnapps is served straight in small glasses and are swallowed in one gulp much like a shot.

Lots of fun to be had with a variety of delicious flavors for toasts and for drinking games.

A BONER

15% alc/vol
1.4 standard drinks

90 ml (3 fl oz) Peach Schnapps
30 ml (1 fl oz) Grenadine

Pour Grenadine into a chilled champagne flute and add Schnapps – do not stir, then serve.

SEX ON THE BEACH IN WINTER

5.7% alc/vol
1 standard drink

23 ml (¾ fl oz) Peach Schnapps
23 ml (¾ fl oz) Vodka
90 ml (3 fl oz) Cranberry Juice
90 ml (3 fl oz) Pineapple Juice
½ teaspoon Coconut Cream

Pour ingredients into a blender over crushed ice and blend until smooth. Pour into a chilled tall glass and serve.

ANDREA'S VIOLENT ORGASM

11.7% alc/vol
2.8 standard drinks

120 ml (4 fl oz) Peach Schnapps
30 ml (1 fl oz) Vodka
150 ml (5 fl oz) Mango Juice

Pour Schnapps and Vodka into a tall glass over ice then stir. Add Juice, stir well and serve.

JUG WOBBLER

11.5% alc/vol
1.8 standard drinks

30 ml (1 fl oz) Apple Schnapps
30 ml (1 fl oz) Gin
15 ml (½ fl oz) Dry Vermouth
8 ml (¼ fl oz) Pernod
120 ml (4 fl oz) Lemonade

Pour Schnapps, Gin, Vermouth and Pernod into a highball glass over ice then stir. Add lemonade, stir gently and serve.

SEX BY
THE LAKE

7.1% alc/vol
1.3 standard drinks

30 ml (1 fl oz) Peach Schnapps
30 ml (1 fl oz) Vodka
90 ml (3 fl oz) Fresh Orange Juice
90 ml (3 fl oz) Pineapple Juice

Pour ingredients into a cocktail shaker over ice and shake. Strain into a chilled highball glass and serve.

SEX IN THE
SHOWER

14% alc/vol
1.7 standard drinks

30 ml (1 fl oz) Butterscotch Schnapps
30 ml (1 fl oz) Blue Curaçao
30 ml (1 fl oz) Triple Sec
60 ml (2 fl oz) Fresh Orange Juice

Pour ingredients into a cocktail shaker over ice and shake. Strain into a chilled champagne flute and serve.

AFFAIR

4.4% alc/vol
0.9 standard drinks

60 ml (2 fl oz) Strawberry Schnapps
60 ml (2 fl oz) Cranberry Juice
60 ml (2 fl oz) Fresh Orange Juice
90 ml (3 fl oz) Soda Water

Pour Schnapps and juices into a highball glass over ice then stir. Add soda, stir gently and serve.

ORANGE CLIMAX

8.2% alc/vol
0.9 standard drinks

30 ml (1 fl oz) Peach Schnapps
15 ml (½ fl oz) Tennessee Whiskey
60 ml (2 fl oz) Pineapple Juice
30 ml (1 fl oz) Fresh Orange Juice
Fresh Whipped Cream

Pour Schnapps, Whiskey and juices into a cocktail shaker over ice. Shake and strain into a chilled old-fashioned glass. Float cream on top and serve.

WILD FLING

4% alc/vol
0.7 standard drinks

45 ml (1½ fl oz) Wildberry Schnapps
120 ml (4 fl oz) Pineapple Juice
60 ml (2 fl oz) Cranberry Juice

Pour ingredients into a cocktail shaker over ice and shake. Strain into a highball glass over ice and serve.

SEX ON THE POOL TABLE

15.5% alc/vol
2 standard drinks

30 ml (1 fl oz) Peach Schnapps
30 ml (1 fl oz) Chambord
30 ml (1 fl oz) Midori
30 ml (1 fl oz) Triple Sec
30 ml (1 fl oz) Grapefruit Juice

Pour ingredients into a cocktail shaker over cracked ice and shake. Pour into a chilled highball glass and serve.

RED-HEADED SLUT

20% alc/vol
1.4 standard drinks

30 ml (1 fl oz) Peach Schnapps
30 ml (1 fl oz) Tennessee Whiskey
30 ml (1 fl oz) Cranberry Juice

Pour ingredients into a mixing glass over ice and stir. Strain into a chilled old-fashioned glass and serve.

SEX ON AN ARIZONA BEACH

5.4% alc/vol
0.5 standard drinks

60 ml (2 fl oz) Peach Schnapps
60 ml (2 fl oz) Vodka
5 ml (⅙ fl oz) Grenadine
Dash of Fresh Lime Juice
Dash of Grapefruit Juice

Pour ingredients into a mixing glass over ice and stir. Strain into a chilled old-fashioned glass over a few ice cubes and serve.

SEX ON THE BEACH – SOUTHERN STYLE

10% alc/vol
0.5 standard drinks

15 ml (½ fl oz) Apple Schnapps
15 ml (½ fl oz) Peach Schnapps
15 ml (½ fl oz) Cranberry Juice
15 ml (½ fl oz) Pineapple Juice

Pour ingredients into a cocktail shaker over ice and shake. Strain into a chilled highball glass and serve.

PINK FETISH

9.5% alc/vol
1.3 standard drinks

30 ml (1 fl oz) Peach Schnapps
30 ml (1 fl oz) Vodka
60 ml (2 fl oz) Cranberry Juice
60 ml (2 fl oz) Fresh Orange Juice
Wedge of Lime

Pour Schnapps, Vodka and juices into a cocktail shaker over ice. Shake and strain into a highball glass over ice. Garnish with a wedge of lime and serve.

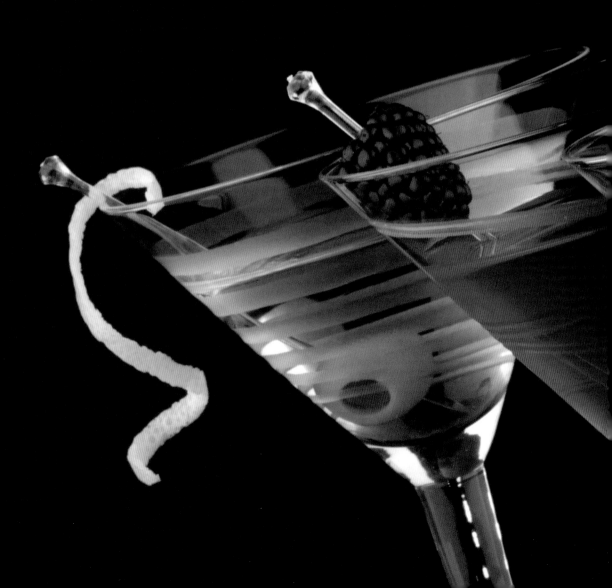

VARIOUS COCKTAILS

Naughty various cocktails include: *Tie Me to the Bedpost* – (submissive and wanting you), *Honeyed Nuts* – (a sticky situation), *Dirty Dancer* – (getting you in the mood) and *Deep Sea Sex* – (hold your breath).

  This section contains a selection of cocktails with base ingredients that have no allocated section in this book such as; Amaretto, Beer, Crème De Cacao, Frangelico, Kahlúa, Malibu, Wine and other liqueurs.

  Various cocktails for various activities and situations.

EROTICA

15.2% alc/vol
2 standard drinks

120 ml (4 fl oz) Champagne
30 ml (1 fl oz) Gin
2 teaspoons Sugar Syrup
8 ml (¼ fl oz) Fresh Lemon Juice
Maraschino Cherry
Slice of Orange

Pour Gin, sugar and juice into a collins glass half filled with ice then stir. Add Champagne and stir gently. Garnish with a cherry and slice of orange then serve.

IN THE SACK

6.4% alc/vol
1.3 standard drinks

90 ml (3 fl oz) Cream Sherry
90 ml (3 fl oz) Fresh Orange Juice
60 ml (2 fl oz) Apricot Nectar
15 ml (½ fl oz) Fresh Lemon Juice
Slice of Orange

Pour Sherry, juices and nectar into a cocktail shaker over ice. Shake and strain into a tall glass over ice. Add a slice of orange and serve.

MUFF DIVER

6.4% alc/vol
0.7 standard drinks

38 ml (1¼ fl oz) White Crème De Cacao
38 ml (1¼ fl oz) Fresh Cream
30 ml (1 fl oz) Fresh Lemon Juice
30 ml (1 fl oz) Fresh Lime Juice

Pour ingredients into a cocktail shaker over ice and shake. Strain into a chilled old-fashioned glass and serve.

DEEP SEA SEX

18.5% alc/vol
0.6 standard drinks

10 ml (⅓ fl oz) Amaretto
10 ml (⅓ fl oz) Blue Curaçao
10 ml (⅓ fl oz) Midori
5 ml (⅙ fl oz) Sweet and Sour Mix
5 ml (⅙ fl oz) Lemonade

Pour Amaretto, Curaçao, Midori and sour mix into a cocktail shaker over cracked ice. Shake and pour into a chilled highball glass. Add lemonade, stir gently and serve.

HEAVENLY ORGASM

23.3% alc/vol
1.1 standard drinks

30 ml (1 fl oz) Frangelico
15 ml (½ fl oz) Amaretto
15 ml (½ fl oz) Bailey's Irish Cream

Pour ingredients into a cocktail shaker over ice and shake. Strain into an old-fashioned glass over ice and serve.

GOOD AS SEX

12.5% alc/vol
3 standard drinks

40 ml (1 fl oz) Blue Curaçao
40 ml (1 fl oz) Passoã
40 ml (1 fl oz) Pisang Ambon
30 ml (1 fl oz) Mandarin Vodka
150 ml (5 fl oz) Lemonade

Pour Curaçao, Passoã, Pisang Ambon and Vodka into a cocktail shaker over ice. Shake and strain into a chilled highball glass. Add lemonade, stir gently and serve.

FLYING MASTURBATOR

9.7% alc/vol
1.4 standard drinks

45 ml (1½ fl oz) Amaretto
23 ml (¾ fl oz) Vodka
100 ml (3 fl oz) Fresh Orange Juice
50 ml (1 fl oz) Cranberry Juice

Pour ingredients into a cocktail shaker over cracked ice and shake. Pour into a chilled highball glass and serve.

BLUE MOVIE

12.6% alc/vol
1.4 standard drinks

30 ml (1 fl oz) Sambuca
15 ml (½ fl oz) Blue Curaçao
15 ml (½ fl oz) Crème De Cassis
40 ml (1 fl oz) Fresh Cream
1 Fresh Egg
Licorice Stick

Pour Sambuca, Curaçao, Cassis, cream and egg into a blender over crushed ice. Blend until smooth and pour into a chilled champagne saucer. Garnish with a licorice stick and serve.

LATIN LOVER

8.8% alc/vol
1.7 standard drinks

90 ml (3 fl oz) Red Wine
45 ml (1½ fl oz) Strawberry Liqueur
105 ml (3½ fl oz) Lemonade

Pour Wine and Liqueur into a chilled tall glass then stir. Add lemonade, stir gently and serve.

BAD GIRL COCKTAIL

10.8% alc/vol
1 standard drink

15 ml (½ fl oz) Malibu
15 ml (½ fl oz) Advocaat
15 ml (½ fl oz) Banana Liqueur
8 ml (¼ fl oz) Galliano
30 ml (1 fl oz) Fresh Cream
½ Banana (diced)

Pour Malibu, Advocaat, Liqueur, Galliano and cream into a blender over crushed ice then add diced banana. Blend until smooth and pour into a chilled champagne saucer then serve.

RED LIGHT

16.6% alc/vol
2 standard drinks

120 ml (4 fl oz) Red Wine
15 ml (½ fl oz) Cointreau
15 ml (½ fl oz) Cordial Médoc
Slice of Lemon

Pour Wine, Cointreau and Médoc into a wine glass over ice then stir. Add a slice of lemon and serve.

ASS GRABBER

14.6% alc/vol
3.8 standard drinks

120 ml (4 fl oz) Beer
90 ml (3 fl oz) Cinnamon Schnapps
60 ml (2 fl oz) Bourbon
15 ml (½ fl oz) Apple Juice
1 Fresh Egg

Pour Schnapps, Bourbon, juice and egg into a cocktail shaker over ice. Shake and strain into a chilled beer glass. Add Beer, stir gently and serve.

PINK PUSSY

12.1% alc/vol
1.7 standard drinks

60 ml (2 fl oz) Campari
30 ml (1 fl oz) Peach Brandy
90 ml (3 fl oz) Bitter-Lemon Soda
Dash of Egg White

Pour Campari, Brandy and egg white into a cocktail shaker over ice. Shake and strain into a highball glass over ice. Add soda, stir gently and serve.

TIE ME TO THE BEDPOST

8.9% alc/vol
1.3 standard drinks

15 ml (½ fl oz) Amaretto
15 ml (½ fl oz) Light Rum
15 ml (½ fl oz) Malibu
15 ml (½ fl oz) Peach Schnapps
60 ml (2 fl oz) Cranberry Juice
60 ml (2 fl oz) Pineapple Juice

Pour ingredients into a cocktail shaker over ice and shake. Strain into a highball glass over ice and serve.

HAWAII ORGASM

15.6% alc/vol
1.6 standard drinks

30 ml (1 fl oz) Malibu
18 ml (⅗ fl oz) Brandy
18 ml (⅗ fl oz) Vodka
30 ml (1 fl oz) Cranberry Juice
30 ml (1 fl oz) Pineapple Juice

Pour ingredients into a cocktail shaker over ice and shake. Strain into a chilled cocktail glass and serve.

STIMULATOR

7% alc/vol
1.6 standard drinks

15 ml (½ fl oz) Kahlúa
15 ml (½ fl oz) Bailey's Irish Cream
15 ml (½ fl oz) Frangelico
15 ml (½ fl oz) Galliano
15 ml (½ fl oz) Tuaca Liqueur
210 ml (7fl oz) Fresh Milk (chilled)

Pour Kahlúa, Bailey's, Frangelico, Galliano and Liqueur into a tall glass over ice then stir. Add milk, stir well and serve.

TATTOOED LOVE GODDESS

12.5% alc/vol
1.2 standard drinks

45 ml (1½ fl oz) Mozart
30 ml (1 fl oz) Vanilla Schnapps
30 ml (1 fl oz) Vodka
15 ml (½ fl oz) Fresh Cream

Pour ingredients into a cocktail shaker over ice and shake. Strain into a chilled cocktail glass and serve.

BELLEVUE GANGBANG

40.8% alc/vol
1.5 standard drinks

23 ml (¾ fl oz) Opal Nera
23 ml (¾ fl oz) Goldschläger

Pour Opal Nera into a chilled liqueur glass and layer Goldschläger on top then serve.

SEX IN THE SUN

14.4% alc/vol
1.4 standard drinks

15 ml (½ fl oz) Galliano
15 ml (½ fl oz) Bacardi
15 ml (½ fl oz) Malibu
15 ml (½ fl oz) Midori
30 ml (1 fl oz) Fresh Lemon Juice
30 ml (1 fl oz) Fresh Orange Juice
Strawberry

Pour Galliano, Bacardi, Malibu, Midori and juices into a cocktail shaker without ice. Shake and pour into a champagne saucer filled with crushed ice. Garnish with a strawberry and serve with 2 short straws.

BIG TITTY DRINK

5.3% alc/vol
1 standard drink

60 ml (2 fl oz) Malibu
180 ml (6 fl oz) Pineapple Juice

Pour ingredients into a mixing glass over ice and stir. Strain into a chilled old-fashioned glass and serve.

HONEYED NUTS

6.1% alc/vol
1 standard drink

30 ml (1 fl oz) Frangelico
15 ml (½ fl oz) Advocaat
15 ml (½ fl oz) Kahlúa
120 ml (4 fl oz) Fresh Cream
30 ml (1 fl oz) Honey
Strawberry

Prepare a brandy balloon with a crushed hazelnut frosted rim – moistened with honey. Pour Frangelico, Advocaat, Kahlúa, cream and honey into a blender over a small amount of crushed ice. Blend and pour into prepared glass. Garnish with a strawberry and serve.

KEEP IT UP

12.4% alc/vol
1.4 standard drinks

90 ml (3 fl oz) Champagne
15 ml (½ fl oz) Cognac
Dash of Angostura Bitters
30 ml (1 fl oz) Fresh Orange Juice
Sugar Cube
Wedge of Orange

Place a sugar cube into a chilled champagne flute. Add Cognac, Bitters and juice then stir. Add Champagne and stir gently. Add a wedge of orange and serve.

BITCHES TIT

2.8% alc/vol
0.4 standard drinks

30 ml (1 fl oz) Chambord
150 ml (5 fl oz) Fresh Cream

Pour ingredients into a cocktail shaker over ice and shake. Strain into a coffee glass half filled with ice and serve.

SCREAMING MULTIPLE ORGASM ON THE BEACH

17.1% alc/vol
2.8 standard drinks

45 ml (1½ fl oz) Amaretto
30 ml (1 fl oz) Malibu
30 ml (1 fl oz) Midori
30 ml (1 fl oz) Peachtree
15 ml (½ fl oz) Triple Sec
60 ml (2 fl oz) Soda Water

Pour Amaretto, Malibu, Midori, Peachtree and
Triple Sec into a cocktail shaker over cracked ice.
Shake and pour into a chilled highball glass.
Add soda, stir gently and serve.

SEX IN THE RED ZONE

15.8% alc/vol
1.5 standard drinks

30 ml (1 fl oz) Sloe Gin
30 ml (1 fl oz) Vodka
60 ml (2 fl oz) Lemonade

Pour Gin and Vodka into a mixing glass over ice.
Stir and strain into a chilled cocktail glass. Add
lemonade, stir gently and serve.

QUICKIE ON THE BAR

35.7% alc/vol
5.2 standard drinks

60 ml (2 fl oz) Everclear
30 ml (1 fl oz) Cherry Liqueur
30 ml (1 fl oz) Grenadine
1 teaspoon Sugar Syrup
60 ml (2 fl oz) Lemonade

Pour Everclear, Liqueur, Grenadine and sugar into
a mixing glass over ice. Stir and strain into a chilled
highball glass. Add lemonade, stir gently and serve.

SMOOTH AND SEXY

12.8% alc/vol
2 standard drinks

50 ml (1 fl oz) Safari Liqueur
20 ml (⅔ fl oz) Amaretto
60 ml (2 fl oz) Fresh Orange Juice
50 ml (1 fl oz) Passion-Fruit Juice
20 ml (⅔ fl oz) Blackberry Juice

Pour ingredients into a cocktail shaker over ice and shake. Strain into a highball glass over ice and serve.

WEIRD WILLY

22.3% alc/vol
3.5 standard drinks

50 ml (1 fl oz) Blue Curaçao
40 ml (1 fl oz) Citrus Vodka
30 ml (1 fl oz) Bacardi
30 ml (1 fl oz) Mango Schnapps
50 ml (1 fl oz) Orange Soda

Pour soda into a chilled highball glass over a few ice cubes. Pour Curaçao, Vodka, Bacardi and Schnapps into a cocktail shaker over ice. Shake and strain into glass over the soda, stir gently then serve.

SWEATY VIRGIN

14.6% alc/vol
2.4 standard drinks

60 ml (2 fl oz) Amaretto
60 ml (2 fl oz) White Crème De Menthe
90 ml (3 fl oz) Lemon-Lime Soda

Pour Amaretto and Crème De Menthe into a cocktail shaker over ice. Shake and strain into a highball glass over crushed ice. Add soda, stir gently and serve.

VOLUPTUOUS

20.4% alc/vol
1.4 standard drinks

40 ml (1 fl oz) Banana Liqueur
23 ml (¾ fl oz) White Tequila
1 teaspoon Sugar Syrup
1 Banana (diced)
Slice of Banana

Pour Liqueur, Tequila and sugar into a blender over crushed ice then add diced banana. Blend until smooth and pour into a chilled old-fashioned glass. Garnish with a slice of banana and serve.

TROPICAL ORGASM

8.9% alc/vol
1.6 standard drinks

60 ml (2 fl oz) Malibu
30 ml (1 fl oz) Triple Sec
135 ml (4½ fl oz) Fresh Orange Juice

Pour ingredients into a cocktail shaker over cracked ice and shake. Pour into a chilled highball glass and serve.

LOST BIKINI

14.8% alc/vol
1.6 standard drinks

23 ml (¾ fl oz) Galliano
23 ml (¾ fl oz) Amaretto
15 ml (½ fl oz) Light Rum
60 ml (2 fl oz) Mandarin Juice
15 ml (½ fl oz) Fresh Lime Juice
2 Cherries

Pour Galliano, Amaretto, Rum and juices into a cocktail shaker over ice. Shake and strain into a chilled cocktail glass. Garnish with cherries and serve.

WITCH'S TIT

16.7% alc/vol
1.2 standard drinks

75 ml (2½ fl oz) Kahlúa
15 ml (½ fl oz) Thick Cream
½ Maraschino Cherry

Pour Kahlúa into a liqueur glass and float cream
on top. Place ½ cherry on cream and serve.

TONGUE STROKE

6.6% alc/vol
1.1 standard drinks

60 ml (2 fl oz) Hard Cider
30 ml (1 fl oz) Brandy
120 ml (4 fl oz) Dry Ginger Ale
Maraschino Cherry

Pour Brandy into a highball glass half filled with
ice and add Cider. Add ginger ale and stir gently.
Garnish with a cherry and serve.

SIT ON MY FACE

20.4% alc/vol
1.4 standard drinks

30 ml (1 fl oz) Kahlúa
30 ml (1 fl oz) Frangelico
30 ml (1 fl oz) Bailey's Irish Cream

Layer ingredients in order given into a liqueur glass and serve.

PINK NIPPLE

4.7% alc/vol
0.9 standard drinks

60 ml (2 fl oz) Raspberry Liqueur
15 ml (½ fl oz) Grenadine
180 ml (6 fl oz) Fresh Cream
Sugar Coated Strawberry

Pour Liqueur and cream into a cocktail shaker over cracked ice. Shake and pour into a chilled hurricane glass. Layer Grenadine on top and garnish with a strawberry then serve.

DIRTY DANCER

12.9% alc/vol
0.7 standard drinks

30 ml (1 fl oz) Dark Crème De Cacao
8 ml (¼ fl oz) White Crème De Menthe
30 ml (1 fl oz) Fresh Cream

Pour ingredients into a cocktail shaker over ice and shake. Strain into a chilled cocktail glass and serve.

MUFF RIDER

8.7% alc/vol
1.6 standard drinks

60 ml (2 fl oz) Sake
30 ml (1 fl oz) Light Rum
90 ml (3 fl oz) Pineapple Juice
90 ml (3 fl oz) Lemon-Lime Soda

Pour Sake, Rum and juice into a cocktail shaker over ice. Shake and strain into a tall glass over ice. Add soda, stir gently and serve.

SEX AT MY HOUSE

9.7% alc/vol
0.8 standard drinks

23 ml (¾ fl oz) Amaretto
23 ml (¾ fl oz) Chambord
60 ml (2 fl oz) Pineapple Juice

Pour ingredients into a cocktail shaker over ice and shake. Strain into a chilled cocktail glass and serve.

TRIPLE XXX

6.5% alc/vol
1 standard drink

30 ml (1 fl oz) Red Curaçao
20 ml (⅔ fl oz) Orange Curaçao
83 ml (2 ¾ fl oz) Apricot Nectar
60 ml (2 fl oz) Passion-Fruit Nectar

Pour ingredients into a cocktail shaker over ice and shake well. Strain into a chilled highball glass and serve.

JUICY LUCI

11.7% alc/vol
1.7 standard drinks

60 ml (2 fl oz) Galliano
120 ml (4 fl oz) Fresh Orange Juice
Slice of Orange

Pour Galliano and juice into a collins glass over ice then stir. Garnish with a slice of orange and serve.

SMOOTH SCREW

12.7% alc/vol
0.8 standard drinks

15 ml (½ fl oz) Tia Maria
15 ml (½ fl oz) Dark Rum
45 ml (1½ fl oz) Pineapple Juice

Pour Tia Maria and juice into a blender over cracked ice. Blend and strain into a chilled cocktail glass. Layer Rum on top and serve.

REARBUSTER

19.4% alc/vol
2.8 standard drinks

60 ml (2 fl oz) Kahlúa
60 ml (2 fl oz) Tequila
60 ml (2 fl oz) Cranberry Juice

Pour ingredients into a highball glass over ice,
stir and serve.

FOREIGN AFFAIR

12.6% alc/vol
2 standard drinks

35 ml (1 ⅙ fl oz) Strawberry Liqueur
30 ml (1 fl oz) Vodka
15 ml (½ fl oz) Cointreau
120 ml (4 fl oz) Fresh Orange Juice

Pour ingredients into a cocktail shaker over ice
and shake. Strain into a highball glass over ice and
serve.

WEEPING ORGASM

20.5% alc/vol
1.5 standard drinks

45 ml (1½ fl oz) Malibu
45 ml (1½ fl oz) Peppermint Schnapps
Wedge of Pineapple

Pour Malibu and Schnapps into a mixing glass over ice. Stir and strain into an old-fashioned glass over crushed ice. Add a wedge of pineapple and serve.

TROPICAL HOOTER PUNCH

12.3% alc/vol
35 standard drinks

1.75 ltr (58 fl oz) Malibu
360 ml (12 fl oz) Midori
750 ml (26 fl oz) Cranberry Juice
750 ml (26 fl oz) Pineapple Juice
Cherries
Slices of Orange

Pour Malibu, Midori and juices into a punch bowl over ice then stir well. Add cherries and slices of orange then serve.

FOREPLAY ON THE NEUTRAL GROUND

10.5% alc/vol
8.9 standard drinks

240 ml (8 fl oz) Vodka
120 ml (4 fl oz) Midori
360 ml (12 fl oz) Cranberry Juice
360 ml (12 fl oz) Pineapple Juice

Pour ingredients into a pitcher over ice and stir well, then serve in glasses filled with ice.

HOT TEMPTATIONS

Naughty hot temptation drinks include: *Hot Dick* – (to warm the girls up), *A Very Sticky Situation* – (fun making that sticky situation) and *Hot Passion* – (keeping the spark alive).

   Hot drinks are perfect on a cool winter's evening to warm you from the inside. For complete satisfaction it is important to only use quality ingredients from the alcohol to the fresh cream, milks and juices. When required to pour boiling water into coffee glasses it is advisable to pour over a silver spoon as this will prevent the glass from cracking.

   With this selection of hot temptations to choose from you should be able to find a drink to warm your desires on those cool winter evenings – from hot coffees and chocolates through to other hot temptations waiting to warm things up.

HOT CREAMY BUSH

6.9% alc/vol
1.3 standard drinks

30 ml (1 fl oz) Irish Whiskey
23 ml (¾ fl oz) Bailey's Irish Cream
180 ml (6 fl oz) Hot Black Coffee

Pour coffee into a coffee glass over a silver spoon
(to prevent glass cracking) and add Whiskey. Add
Bailey's, stir and serve.

HOT PLEASURE

7.4% alc/vol
1.2 standard drinks

30 ml (1 fl oz) Bourbon
10 ml (⅓ fl oz) Amaretto
150 ml (5 fl oz) Hot Black Coffee
Sugar to Taste
Fresh Whipped Cream
Grated Chocolate

Pour coffee into a coffee glass over a silver spoon
(to prevent glass cracking) then add Bourbon and
Amaretto. Add sugar to taste and stir. Float cream on
top and sprinkle chocolate over cream then serve.

A VERY STICKY SITUATION

12.7% alc/vol
1.7 standard drinks

53 ml (1¾ fl oz) Dark Crème De Cacao
23 ml (¾ fl oz) Goldschläger
75 ml (2½ fl oz) Hot Cocoa
23 ml (¾ fl oz) Honey

Pour hot cocoa into a coffee glass over a silver spoon (to prevent glass cracking) then add Cacao and Goldschläger. Add honey, stir well and serve.

HOT DICK

13.7% alc/vol
2.7 standard drinks

60 ml (2 fl oz) Bailey's Irish Cream
60 ml (2 fl oz) Grand Marnier
120 ml (4 fl oz) Hot Black Coffee
Fresh Whipped Cream
Grated Chocolate

Pour coffee into a coffee glass over a silver spoon (to prevent glass cracking) and add Bailey's. Add Grand Marnier and stir. Float cream on top and sprinkle chocolate over the cream then serve.

ALLISON'S BUTTER BLOW JOB

11.9% alc/vol
3.5 standard drinks

250 ml (8 fl oz) Cider
90 ml (3 fl oz) Dark Rum
2 tablespoons Butter

Pour Cider and Rum into a saucepan. Heat to a simmer without boiling whilst stirring occasionally and add butter then stir to dissolve. Remove from heat and pour into a pre-warmed mug over a silver spoon (to prevent glass cracking) then serve.

BEDROOM FARCE

11.1% alc/vol
1.6 standard drinks

30 ml (1 fl oz) Dark Rum
15 ml (½ fl oz) Bourbon
10 ml (⅓ fl oz) Galliano
120 ml (4 fl oz) Hot Cocoa
Fresh Whipped Cream
Grated Chocolate

Pour hot cocoa into a coffee glass over a silver spoon (to prevent glass cracking) and add Rum. Add Bourbon and Galliano then stir. Float cream on top and sprinkle chocolate over cream then serve.

OH!!! BABY

4.6% alc/vol
0.9 standard drinks

30 ml (1 fl oz) Bailey's Irish Cream
30 ml (1 fl oz) Butterscotch Schnapps
180 ml (6 fl oz) Boiling Water

Pour boiling water into a coffee glass over a silver spoon (to prevent glass cracking) and add Bailey's. Add Schnapps, stir and serve.

HOT KISS

7.6% alc/vol
1.5 standard drinks

30 ml (1 fl oz) Irish Whiskey
15 ml (½ fl oz) White Crème De Cacao
15 ml (½ fl oz) White Crème De Menthe
180 ml (6 fl oz) Hot Black Coffee
Fresh Whipped Cream
Grated Chocolate

Pour coffee into a coffee glass over a silver spoon (to prevent glass cracking) and add Whiskey. Add Cacao and Crème De Menthe then stir. Float cream on top and sprinkle chocolate over cream then serve.

FLORI'S HOT TUB HEAVEN

12.4% alc/vol
2.3 standard drinks

30 ml (1 fl oz) Amaretto
30 ml (1 fl oz) Peppermint Schnapps
90 ml (3 fl oz) Bailey's Irish Cream
90 ml (3 fl oz) Hot Black Coffee

Pour ingredients in order given into a coffee glass – do not stir, then serve with a swizzle stick.

JEN'S CREAMY SIGHS

7.1% alc/vol
1.4 standard drinks

30 ml (1 fl oz) Amaretto
30 ml (1 fl oz) Bailey's Irish Cream
10 ml (⅓ fl oz) Grand Marnier
165 ml (5½ fl oz) Hot Black Coffee
Sugar to Taste
Fresh Whipped Cream

Pour coffee into a coffee glass over a silver spoon (to prevent glass cracking) then add Amaretto and Bailey's. Add sugar to taste and stir. Float cream on top and add Grand Marnier by pouring over cream then serve with a swizzle stick.

HOT PASSION

9.3% alc/vol
1.7 standard drinks

45 ml (1½ fl oz) Passion-Fruit Liqueur
30 ml (1 fl oz) Grand Marnier
150 ml (5 fl oz) Hot Black Coffee

Pour coffee into a coffee glass over a silver spoon (to prevent glass cracking) then add Liqueur and stir. Layer Grand Marnier on top and serve.

DOT'S HOT SPOT

2.3% alc/vol
0.3 standard drinks

90 ml (3 fl oz) Dry Cider
90 ml (3 fl oz) White Grape Juice
1 teaspoon Honey
Cinnamon Stick
Slice of Lemon

Pour Cider, juice and honey into a saucepan then add remaining ingredients. Heat to a simmer whilst stirring frequently then remove from heat. Strain into a goblet over a silver spoon (to prevent glass cracking) and serve.

NON-ALCOHOLIC

Naughty non-alcohol drinks include: *Blast Off!* – (after your ignition has been lit) and *Afterglow* – (final stage of satisfaction).

Non-alcoholic drinks or "mocktails" as they are often referred to, are the perfect drinks for those who choose not to consume alcohol, whether it is because they have to drive or any number of other reasons which should be respected without pressure or question.

These drinks could be a substitute for alcohol drinks towards the end of your night, especially if you have plans on performing other bedroom activities and don't want to be lacking in certain areas!

PUSSY FRUIT

60 ml (2 fl oz) Fresh Orange Juice
30 ml (1 fl oz) Grenadine
1 Fresh Egg
6 Pieces of Pineapple
3 Strawberries
½ Peach (diced)

Pour juice, Grenadine and egg into a blender
over crushed ice then add remaining ingredients.
Blend until smooth and pour into a chilled tall glass
then serve.

SAFE SEX ON THE BEACH

90 ml (3 fl oz) Fresh Orange Juice
90 ml (3 fl oz) Pineapple Juice
30 ml (1 fl oz) Peach Nectar
8 ml (¼ fl oz) Grenadine

Pour ingredients into a cocktail shaker over ice and
shake. Strain into a highball glass half filled with ice
and serve.

BLAST OFF!

150 ml (5 fl oz) Cranberry Juice
75 ml (2½ fl oz) Soda Water
75 ml (2½ fl oz) Fresh Orange Juice

Build ingredients into a chilled collins glass over
a few ice cubes then serve with a swizzle stick and
2 straws.

AFTERGLOW

90 ml (3 fl oz) Fresh Orange Juice
90 ml (3 fl oz) Pineapple Juice
23 ml (¾ fl oz) Grenadine

Pour ingredients into a mixing glass over ice and
stir. Strain into a highball glass over ice and serve.

GLOSSARY

	% alc/vol	
Advocaat	18	Dutch Brandy-based liqueur produced from egg yolk and sugar.
Amaretto	28	Almond-flavor liqueur that originated from Italy in 1525.
Angostura Bitters	45	Produced with infusions of herbs; it is the Bitters that gives Pink Gin its color.
Applejack	40	Apple-flavor Brandy produced in America.
Apricot Brandy	23	Apricot-flavor Brandy.
Bacardi	37.5	Brand name of a Light Rum produced in Cuba.
Bacardi Limon Rum	35	Citrus-flavor Bacardi Rum produced with oils from lemons, limes and grapefruits.
Bailey's Irish Cream	17	Brand name of a slight chocolate-flavor Irish cream liqueur produced with a blend of Irish Whiskey and cream.
Banana Liqueur	23	Banana-flavor liqueur.
Beer	5	Produced from fermentation of cereals and flavored with hops.
Bénédictine (D.O.M)	40	Cognac-based sweet herb-flavor liqueur originally created in 1510 by the Benedictine monks, making it one of the world's oldest liqueurs.

Blackberry Brandy	35	Blackberry-flavor Brandy distilled from blackberries.
Bourbon	40	Sweet Whiskey distilled from corn and produced in America.
Brandy	37	Distilled spirit fermented from grapes. If other fruits are used it must be stated on the bottle's label.
Campari	25	Bitter and dry red apéritif Wine produced in Italy.
Canadian Whisky	38	Delicately flavored, mild and light bodied Whisky that is produced mainly from corn with proportions of rye, wheat and barley malt.
Chambord	16.5	Black raspberry-flavor liqueur produced in the Burgundy region of France.
Champagne	12	Sparkling Wine that is produced in the Champagne region of France.
Chartreuse (Yellow)	40	Herbal liqueur produced in France.
Cherry Brandy	23	Cherry-flavor Brandy.
Cherry Liqueur	30	Cherry-flavor liqueur.
Cider	4.7	Fermented apple juice.
Citrus Vodka	35	Citrus twist-flavor Vodka.
Coconut Liqueur	23	Coconut-flavor liqueur with a Light Rum-base.
Cognac	40	Fine Brandy produced in France, no other country is permitted to label their Brandy as Cognac.

Cointreau	40	Sweet orange-flavor liqueur that is colorless and arguably the world's finest Triple Sec. It has been produced by the Cointreau family in France since 1849.
Cordial Médoc	38	Cordial liqueur version of Médoc Wine.
Crème De Cacao	23	Chocolate and vanilla-flavor liqueur produced from cocoa beans, vanilla and spices. It is available in two varieties: dark and white (clear).
Crème De Cassis	20	Blackcurrant-flavor liqueur.
Crème De Menthe	23	Peppermint-flavor liqueur produced in three varieties: green, red and white (clear).
Curaçao	25	Sweet orange-flavor liqueur produced from curaçao orange peel. It is available in six varieties: blue, green, orange, red, white (clear) and yellow.
Drambuie	40	Scotch Whisky-based liqueur flavored from heather honey and herbs.
Dubonnet	16	Red Wine-based Vermouth apéritif produced in France and originally created by Joseph Dubonnet in 1846.
Everclear	95	Pure grain alcohol spirit that is also available at 75% alc/vol. For recipes containing this spirit have been calculated at 95% alc/vol.
Finlandia Vodka	40	Vodka produced in Finland.
Forbidden Fruit	35	Brandy-based liqueur flavored with sweet orange and grapefruit with a slightly

bitter aftertaste. It is produced in America and has a reddish orange color.

Frangelico	24	Hazelnut-flavor liqueur created by a monk over 300 years ago in the Piedmont region of Italy.
Galliano	35	Aniseed and licorice-flavor liqueur with a distinctive yellow color. Produced in Italy from over 80 berries, herbs and roots.
Gin	37	Colorless spirit produced from juniper berries and other botanicals. Gin is the most widely required spirit in cocktails.
Goldschläger	43.5	Clear cinnamon-flavor Schnapps liqueur containing 24K gold flakes combined with the spirit.
Grand Marnier	40	Orange-flavor Cognac-based liqueur produced in France and created in 1880. It is available in two varieties: red ribbon and yellow ribbon – red ribbon has a higher % alc/vol at 40% alc/vol.
Grenadine	Nil	Sweet red syrup, flavored with pomegranate juice.
Irish Mist	40	Irish Whiskey-based liqueur flavored with herbs and honey.
Jägermeister	35	Herb liqueur produced in Germany from 56 herbs, fruits and roots. Originally created in 1934 by Curt Mast and the recipe still remains a secret.

Kahlúa	20	Coffee-flavor liqueur produced in Mexico.
Malibu	21	Coconut-flavor liqueur with a Light Jamaica Rum-base. This sweet clear liqueur is produced in Barbados.
Maraschino Liqueur	40	Cherry-flavor clear liqueur that originated in Italy.
Midori	21	Brand name of a honeydew melon-flavor liqueur that is green in color and produced by the Suntory Distilling Company in Japan.
Mozart	20	Chocolate-flavor cream liqueur produced in Austria.
Opal Nera	38	Brand name of an aniseed-flavor Black Sambuca.
Orange Bitters	26	Orange-flavor liqueur that is bitter-sweet and dry. It is produced from the peel of seville oranges.
Orgeat	Nil	Almond-flavor syrup.
Ouzo	37	Aniseed-flavor spirit distilled from anise seeds, berries, herbs and pressed grapes. Originally produced in Greece.
Parfait Amour	23	Citrus and rose scented, violet color liqueur. Produced from Brandy, citrus and herbs it originated from France.
Passoã	20	Passion-fruit-flavor liqueur produced from passion-fruit.
Peachtree	23	Clear peach-flavor liqueur.

Pernod	40	Aniseed-flavor liqueur originally produced in France as a substitute for Absinthe.
Pisang Ambon	21	Banana and herb-flavor liqueur originating from Indonesia and is produced from the tropical fruits and herbs of South-East Asia.
Port	18	Fortified Wine: Ruby – dark and rough, Tawny – smoother and dry Vintage Port – not a blend and aged in wooden barrels.
Quetsch	40	Plum-flavor clear Brandy produced from black grapes.
Raspberry Liqueur	20	Raspberry-flavor liqueur.
Rum	37	Spirit distilled from sugar cane syrup, there are many varieties of Rum worldwide.
Rum (Dark)	37	Spirit is aged in wooden barrels for between three and twelve years with the addition of caramel added in some cases to darken the spirit. Dark Rum varieties include: Jamaica, Haiti and Martinique Rums.
Rum (Golden)	37	Spirit aged in charred barrels for three years to produce a golden color.
Rum (Light)	38	Spirit aged for approximately six to twelve months in oak casks after being distilled in a column-still which produces clear spirit. Originally produced in the southern Caribbean Islands.
Rumplemintz	50	Peppermint-flavor Schnapps produced in Germany.

Safari	20	Liqueur distilled from exotic fruits.
Sake	15.5	Japanese brew fermented from rice, it may be served chilled or warm.
Sambuca	38	Aniseed-flavor liqueur produced from aniseed, herbs and roots. This liqueur is produced in Italy.
Schnapps	20	Generic name for flavored alcohol produced from grain or potato mash. Schnapps can be very sweet through to dry with many varieties available. % alc/vol content varies, 20% alc/vol is average for commercial Schnapps.
Sherry	18	Produced from grapes and fortified with Brandy. True Sherry originates from Jerez in southern Spain.
Sloe Gin	26	Sweet Gin-based liqueur that is flavored with sloe plums (blackthorn plums).
Southern Comfort	37	Peach-flavor liqueur that is Brandy and Bourbon-based. Created by M.W. Heron in New Orleans over one hundred years ago.
Spiced Rum	35	Blended with a variety of spices.
Strawberry Liqueur	23	Strawberry-flavor liqueur.
Tequila	38	Spirit distilled from the sap of the dessert dwelling agave plant in Mexico.
Tia Maria	26.5	Coffee-flavor Rum-based Jamaican liqueur.

Triple Sec	25	Orange-flavor liqueur produced from orange peel – also referred to as Curaçao.
Tuaca Liqueur	35	Light sweet liqueur with a citrus and vanilla character produced in Italy.
Vermouth (Dry)	18	A Fortified Wine-based apéritif produced from herbs, flowers and roots.
Vodka	37	Clear, odourless and tasteless spirit distilled from fermented grain mash and filtered through charcoal. Traditional Russian and Polish Vodkas have subtle aromas and flavors.
Whisky	40	Spirit distilled from grain and then aged. They are produced in blends and single malts.
Wild Turkey Bourbon	43.4	Brand name of a Kentucky Bourbon.
Yukon Jack	50	Brand name of a sweet herb liqueur produced in Canada.

INDEX

First published in 2015 by New Holland Publishers Pty Ltd
London • Sydney • Auckland

The Chandlery Unit 704 50 Westminster Bridge Road London SE1 7QY United Kingdom
1/66 Gibbes Street Chatswood NSW 2067 Australia
5/39 Woodside Ave Northcote, Auckland 0627 New Zealand

www.newhollandpublishers.com

A record of this book is held at the British Library and the National Library of Australia.

ISBN 9781742577746

Managing Director: Fiona Schultz
Publisher: Diane Ward
Project Editor: Holly Willsher
Designer: Kathie Baxter Eastway
Cover Design: Lorena Susak
Production Director: Olga Dementiev
Printer: Toppan Leefung Printing Limited
10 9 8 7 6 5 4 3 2 1

Keep up with New Holland Publishers on Facebook
www.facebook.com/NewHollandPublishers